BRIDGE FOR WOMEN

BRIDGE
FOR
WOMEN

by

Peggy Solomon

Rixi Markus

Mary Jane Farell

Bee Gale Schenken

Helen Sobel Smith

Edited by Richard L. Frey
Editor, the Official Encyclopedia of Bridge

Doubleday & Company Inc.
Garden City, New York

A Rutledge Book

BRIDGE
FOR
WOMEN

Contents

INTRODUCTION, page 8
by Richard L. Frey

Peggy Solomon on
Opening Bid and Response: the Basis
of Partnership
How to exploit the feminine advantage
women enjoy as good partners, page 11

Quizzes, page 37

Rixi Markus on
The Art of the Overcall
A brilliant analysis of competitive bidding
in which women lose points by not
bidding enough, and men lose them
by bidding too much, page 43

Quizzes, page 81

Mary Jane Farell on
The Precarious Preempt
How women can overcome their bargain-hunting
instincts and make the preemptive
bids that pay off, page 95

Quizzes, page 117

Bee Gale Schenken on
Female Intuition: What's It Worth?
**Men who have it call it "table presence"; women
have ESP naturally, but don't know
how to make the most of it, page 123**

Quizzes, page 153

Helen Sobel Smith on
How to Play Bridge With a Man
**How to play with a Goren . . . and some
inside tips on how to play the Goren point count
when you are defending. A unique chapter including
some little-known facts on how experts think when
they play defense, page 161**

Quizzes, page 196

BIDDING VALUATION AT A GLANCE, page 204

CONVENTIONS, page 205

QUESTIONS OF BRIDGE LAW, page 210

EXTRACTS FROM THE LAWS OF BRIDGE, page 213

Introduction

When an orator in the French Chamber of Deputies observed, "Between men and women, there is a difference!" the gallant Chamber arose to a man and cried, "Vive la différence!"

This is a bridge book with a difference. It is the first book ever to recognize that there is a difference between the male and the female approach to the game, and to tell the reader how to minimize the disadvantages under which women labor and how to make capital out of the natural advantages women bring to the bridge table. It is the first bridge book ever to present the advice and experience of five different experts—all of them women.

This is not a book for brand new players. It assumes that you know the mechanics of the game, that you already have a bridge system and that you have played enough so *that you want to play better. Then it shows you how.*

You will find in this book some ideas that you have never seen explained before—ideas like Helen Sobel Smith's revealing discussion of how to use the point count, not in your bidding but in your defensive play; ideas like Rixi Markus' advice on when not to be a blabbermouth; Peggy Solomon's tips on how to get the most out of any partner; Bee Schenken's graphic and practical revelations about making use of the intuition—the ESP—that most women have but don't know how to use; Mary Jane Farell's caution about being an economist when the situation calls for spendthrift tactics.

I think this is a book you will enjoy reading. I know you will enjoy it more when you start using it in your own table tactics and find how much it will help you to win.

Peggy Solomon

Member, victorious 1966 U.S. World Olympiad Pairs squad

With some 5,000 master points and no fewer than ten national championship titles to her credit, Peggy Solomon has ranked among the top five women of bridge for more than twenty-five years. The first of Peggy's ten national championship victories came in 1942—the Fall National Women's team title, which she won again in 1957 and again in 1963. She has also won the Lebhar trophy for the National Mixed team championship three times. One of her most recent triumphs understandably brought her a great deal of pride. Her third place finish in the 1966 World Pair Olympic with Mary Jane Farell helped to clinch for the United States the Charles J. Solomon Trophy established by her husband as the award to the nation with the best combined result in the Olympic Open Pair, Women's Pair and Mixed Pair events.

Charles Solomon's career in world bridge has been tremendously successful both as a top-ranked player and an executive officer. Peggy has shared both careers with the skill and charm that have made her America's goodwill ambassadress of bridge.

No part of the game, she says, is more important than partnership, and this is the factor in which women naturally excel. Her chapter is the most revealing view of fundamentals that has ever been included in a bridge book.

Opening Bid and Response: the Basis of Partnership

**Basis of winning partnership—
exploiting the advantage of being
a woman ... by Peggy Solomon**

Women do not, as a rule, have the intense drive to take command that is a bridge disadvantage to men. Our instinct in any endeavor is to make decisions in collaboration with a partner. In bridge, this can be a powerful weapon for reaching profitable decisions based on the clearest possible exchange of information. The cornerstone of that exchange is the sound opening bid.

The perfect partner, according to a cynic's definition, is one who stands by you through all the troubles you wouldn't have gotten into without him. Sharply etched in the acid of this bitter truth is a pointer toward successful bridge partnership: never lose sight of what *you* have contributed to the downfall.

The most successful team in all bridge history, Italy's famed Blue Team, includes some of the world's great individual stars. But the same is true of many of the teams they defeated during their domination of world championship play that began in 1957. What the Blue Team enjoyed more than did any other team is rapport.

In part this has been due to team rules that bar discussion of hands until after the play; that forbid partners from holding partnership discussions except in a privacy that excludes even their teammates. In part, it is because the Italian systems—each pair plays a different one—impose the kind of discipline that is the key to good partnership.

Relax. I am *not* going to suggest that you learn an Italian system, or that what I can tell you here will make you a world champion. My point is merely that, in bridge, being a good partner can definitely win more for you than any other single skill in the game.

Yes, bridge partnership is a skill. Any bridge system is primarily a basis for partnership. And women are fortunate that teamwork counts so much, because it is so much easier and more natural for them to be good partners.

As an example, let me cite an incident that took place early in my tournament career. Against two aggressive male opponents, as dealer I happened to pick out of the duplicate board the following hand:

♠ K J 9 6 4 ♡ A Q J 3 ◇ Q J 10 ♣ 8

Both sides were vulnerable. I opened one spade and, after a pass, my partner responded one notrump. I bid two hearts, which sailed around to my right-hand opponent who reopened with a bid of two spades. I remember thinking, "Here's my chance to teach a lesson to a wise guy who thinks he can take advantage of a couple of women." But just before I uttered a scornful "Double," a thought struck me. My hand was no better than shown by the bids I had already made. My partner knew I had a sound bid and a five-card spade suit (we were playing a system that doesn't permit opening four-card majors). So why shouldn't I let her decide what to do next? I passed and, to my disappointment, so did she. I recovered when the hand was over, because this was the layout:

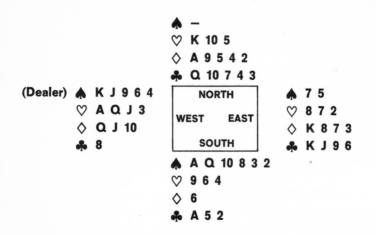

I led the diamond queen, won by dummy's ace. Declarer ruffed a diamond and led a heart, winning my jack with dummy's king. After ruffing another diamond, South cashed the club ace and exited with a heart, snaring me in an end play. I took home two heart tricks and unwisely led a fourth round, hoping that partner could produce an uppercut with a high trump. But South topped her seven with his eight and his lead of a losing club found me unable to do anything but ruff and lead spades up to declarer's ace-queen-ten. This process was repeated after I trumped still another club lead and so South made not just two spades but three.

Yes, I could have saved the overtrick by leading a trump instead of the fourth heart. When South got out with a club, I'd have a heart to discard and East could lead a trump through. But what I had lost in the play I had more than made up by saying "Pass" instead of "Double." We got quite a good score because so many West players treated the spade bid by South as an insult which it was their mission in life to avenge, *alone*. I had made a momentous discovery: that there are many hands with which it is best to let partner make the decision.

Then and there, I resolved to build my game on the partnership principle. I toss my problems into partner's lap whenever it appears that partner might be in the best position to solve them.

Let me hasten to add that I try never to leave it to partner when I think I can solve her problems or prevent a problem from arising. Especially when playing with a male partner, it is important for a woman not to dodge her share of the responsibility.

The Opening Bid

Since this isn't a primer for beginners, I assume that you are acquainted with the basic fundamentals of bridge: point count, opening bid requirements, how tricks are won at both trump and notrump contracts. Presumably you have learned the basic elements of a system and, since it is the one most people play and therefore the one that is most desirable for you to know, I assume that system is what is known as "Standard American."* You require 13 points for a minimum opening bid; your notrump ranges from 16 to 18; there is no taboo on opening bids in four-card majors; responder keeps the bidding open with 6 points or more; he needs 10 points or more to bid a new suit at the two-level. With a hand so powerful that game is likely even if partner holds fewer than 6 points, opener makes a forcing bid of two in a suit to which partner makes a negative response of two notrump if he holds less than a trick and a half in high cards, or a trick plus in a hand with a good five-card suit.

But this is not what I mean when I speak of a firm foundation; your system is more like the plot of ground on which the building foundation will be laid and the bidding structure reared. The essential requirement of the foundation is a sound opening bid. A sound opening one-bid is never less than 13 points, of which at least 10 or 11 should be in solid high-card values. A man will often decide to open with less. The decision may be based on his conviction that he is a genius; or he liked the shape of the hand; or he had a hunch; or he must prove he is brave; or he doesn't like

---

With many partners, I play a system that demands supersound opening bids in first or second seat and does not permit opening in a major suit of less than five cards. But I don't propose to argue the merits of this system against "standard."

being bound by silly rules; or he didn't feel like passing. He may even argue that half the time these bids pay off, as against the other half when they get him into trouble. What he forgets to count are the invisible losses that occur because his partner can never be sure that he actually has his full requirements.

I recommend that you leave genius bids to the man. **If you hold 12 points or less, pass.**

On the other hand, you should never fail to open when you have 14 points or more. Sure, it's nice sometimes to surprise everybody when you back into the bidding later and it turns out that you have passed a big hand. But nobody is likely to be more surprised than your partner. It is so much simpler to play with a partner you can rely on to pass with 12 points or fewer and to bid with 14 or more.

By sticking to the "never on 12" and "always on 14" rules, you not only improve the accuracy of partnership bidding; you also make possible the keenest kind of defense.

The hand that falls between the two "rules"—the 13-pointer —can sometimes be a problem. Since there are 13-point bids and 13-point passes, you have to have some way of distinguishing between them. I offer two easy rules: Open any 13-pointer that offers an easy rebid, and with which a bid gives your partner helpful information as to the location of your strength. Pass if your rebid can be a headache, or if your first bid may mislead partner.

Specifically:

(a) ♠ A J 7 6 ♡ 7 3 ◇ Q 8 2 ♣ K Q 9 5
(b) ♠ A 6 ♡ Q 7 5 3 ◇ 7 5 2 ♣ A Q 4 2
(c) ♠ Q 5 4 3 ♡ Q 5 4 3 ◇ A K ♣ J 9 3
(d) ♠ Q 5 4 3 ♡ Q 5 4 3 ◇ 6 5 ♣ A K J

(a) Open with one club. If partner responds in a red suit,

you can rebid one spade. If he bids spades, you raise; if he bids no-trump or raises clubs, you pass.

(b) Pass. A heart opening bid would mislead partner; a club opening bid would find your hand devalued below 13 points if you had to rebid one notrump over one spade, not to mention the fact that your diamond suit is woefully weak.

(c) Pass. Neither of your major suits is biddable and a three-card minor-suit bid of one club cannot support an opening lead of the suit if the opponents become declarer.

(d) Bid one club. As defender, you will welcome a club lead. If partner responds in either major, you can raise; if he bids one diamond you can bid one notrump, or, if your style requires that one notrump would deny a four-card major, you can rebid one heart. Finally, if he responds one notrump, he should have at least 9 to 10 points in high cards and one notrump should be a comfortable contract.

Thus far, we have been talking about opening bids when partner has not yet passed. In third or fourth seat, however, when it is not required that you rebid over any possible one-over-one or two-over-one response, different considerations come into the reckoning. The decision whether to open a borderline hand often depends on the major-suit holdings. Example:

♠ J 6 4 ♡ J 3 ◇ K Q 7 5 ♣ A J 6 2

With such poor holdings in the major suits, it is wise to pass this hand; even if the opponents do not have enough points to open the bidding, there is a big danger they might buy the contract in a major suit if *you* open. But if the major and minor suits were reversed it would be safe to open, since there would be little danger that the deal belonged to the opposition.

While we are on this important topic of major-suit holdings, here is a tip that can help you to add the touch of dash and daring that amateur male psychologists claim women don't possess. Suppose that after three passes you hold the following:

♠ — ♡ Q J 8 3 2 ◇ 10 9 5 3 ♣ A K 9 8

Because this hand contains a spade void, many players would throw it in, arguing that the opposition must hold a string of spades and will surely compete for the partial if the bidding is opened. But it isn't so simple; the very fact that there have been three passes means it is highly unlikely that any one player holds a corner on spades. The most likely round-the-table distribution of that suit is 5-4-4-0, so even if the opposition hold nine spades between them, they'll have plenty of trouble making a partial on a trump suit that breaks 4-0.

It would be far more likely the opponent could make a spade partial if you and your partner held two spades each instead of four in one hand and none in the other, so it is a fair gamble to venture one heart on this hand. Although it is quite possible the opposition may eventually buy the contract in spades, the odds are they will fail to make their partial.

This same principle—bidding bolder just *because* you are very short of the suit that the enemy may be long on—can be utilized in many other situations. Properly handled, it can give your bidding style a blend of discretion and adventurousness, and help make you a truly formidable adversary.

Biddable suits   Consistency in bidding is by far the easiest way to save your partner headaches. As well as keeping a strict eye on the *strength* of my opening bids, I am rather particular about the texture of the *suit* I bid, and I seldom open a four-card major unless it includes at least four high-card points. Example:

♠ Q 8 6 ♡ K 8 3 2 ◇ K 9 4 ♣ A Q 10

Since the hearts are not quite biddable, I would open one club. However, with *two* four-card majors, a discreet relaxation of the rules may be in order.

♠ K 10 6 4   ♡ A J 8 2   ◇ A Q 4   ♣ 9 6

Major suits are a valuable asset even if, as in this instance, they are somewhat spindly. When one is fortunate enough to hold two such suits it is advisable to make sure they get bid. On this particular hand the heart suit contains five points and is therefore biddable, but unfortunately it is standard procedure to open the *higher-ranking* of two touching suits and it would be unwise to depart from that principle here. Therefore the recommended opening bid is one spade, even though this suit contains only three high-card points.

Incidentally, it would also be possible to open one diamond on the above hand—the stronger minor suit—and this would indeed be the solution if the spades and hearts were somewhat weaker. The short diamond isn't used as often as the short club opening, but it is entirely permissible.

Away from the bridge table, I'm as fond of surprises as anyone, but when I get into a bridge game my aim is to shield partner from shocks. I have found that the less surprised my partner is when she sees the dummy, the more likely it is we have reached the correct contract. Here are some more opening-bid hints that will help keep your partner's eyebrows where they belong.

Notrump openings are the most descriptive of all bids, flashing to partner in a single bid an exact picture of your point count and balanced distribution. Furthermore, an opening notrump bid takes care of the hand with which it would be most troublesome to know the correct rebid if you chose some other opening.

The perfect set-up for a notrump hand includes 16-18 high-card points; plentiful tenace or king holdings that you would prefer to have led up to rather than led through; balanced distribution and no unstopped suit. But if you wait for exactly this hand, you would almost never get a one-notrump bid. Do not hesitate to open one notrump with a hand that includes all but one of the desired features. In fact, you might well widen the range of your notrump bid so that it may go as low as 15 points (all in high cards, of course) and either keep the upper limit at 18 or reduce it to 17. The criterion should be the number of honor cards included to make up the total—the more honors, the more suitable the hand for notrump play. Thus,

♠ A 8 7   ♡ A 8 7   ◇ A 8 7   ♣ K 8 7 5

counts 15 points, but is better opened with one club. And

♠ A K 7   ♡ A 8 7   ◇ A 8 7   ♣ K 8 7 2

counts 18 points but is also better opened with one club. *The ideal notrump bid has about seven honor cards.* On this basis, the 15-point hand above is too weak.

When a hand counts 18 points with only five honor cards, the fact that it is made up of first- or second-round controls and few intermediates makes it more valuable for play at a suit. Another factor that eliminates many of the hands that count 18 points in high cards is that they include a doubleton and therefore take an additional distributional point which lifts them out of the notrump range.

The notrump opening is recommended for each of these example hands despite the flaw that makes them not exactly perfect notrump bids:

(a) ♠ J 5   ♡ A Q 10   ◇ K 10 7 2   ♣ A Q 10 3

With a 16 count and several tenace holdings—i.e., honor combinations that are more likely to win tricks if they are led up to—this is essentially a one-notrump bid, even though it contains a weak doubleton.

(b) ♠ J 8 6 4 3   ♡ K J 3   ◇ A Q   ♣ A J 9

Although any five-card suit is biddable, *you don't have to bid every five-card suit you pick up, even when it is a five-card major.* The desirability of having the tenaces led up to is important. Even more so is the need to solve the rebid problem that is created if you open with one spade.

(c) ♠ A 10 4   ♡ A 10 2   ◇ A 9 7 2   ♣ A 9 7

Add a point for the holding of all four aces and this hand is still worth only 17 and is best opened with one notrump, although it does not contain any tenace holdings.

(d) ♠ Q 9 7 6   ♡ Q 9 7 6   ◇ A Q   ♣ A Q J

No need to worry about missing a fit in one of the four-card majors since, after you open with one notrump, partner can help to locate a four-four fit by a Stayman* two-club response.

Avoid a notrump bid with a holding that includes more than one flaw. For example:

♠ 9 7 6 5   ♡ J 6 3   ◇ A K J   ♣ A Q J

The count is right and your hand is balanced, but you have two unstopped suits. Whenever 16 or more points are largely concentrated in two suits, and especially in two short suits, find some other bid. Either one club or one diamond is right for this hand.

---

*See Stayman Convention description, page 209.

I have suggested adding one point to your notrump range—but not without the advice and consent of your partner. Whatever you agree your notrumps are to be, stick to your agreement.

Opening forcing bids In its simplest original form, an opening bid of two in a suit forces partner to respond until game (or a satisfactory penalty double of the opponents) has been reached. This is the bid that tends to be most abused by the opener and—perhaps as a consequence—often flouted by the responder. For this reason, I urge you to set your standard requirements with your partner and, no matter what the temptation, do not depart from them. If your system calls for you to keep responding, don't pass, no matter how weak your hand.

The standard guideline for a forcing suit two-bid is 24 points with a strong six-card suit (or with a five-card suit plus a four-card suit) and 25 points with a strong five-card suit. With 25-27 points in high cards and flat distribution, you open with three no-trump; with 22-24 points, open with two notrump. Neither of these bids is forcing.

The lower you set the standards for these strength-showing bids, the more often you get a chance to use them, but you cannot lower the standards on the spur of the moment because you feel the urge to make a two-bid on that particular hand.

One requirement that you *can* ease in order to expand the range of two-bid hands is that partner must bid to game. You can open a two-bid with a somewhat weaker one-suited hand if you agree that partner, having dutifully responded two notrump to indicate his weakness, may pass the next time if you make a simple rebid of the same suit: two hearts, two notrump, three hearts. You might hold:

♠ A J 9   ♡ A K Q 10 8 7   ◇ A J 10   ♣ 2

This hand counts to only 21 points and with bad breaks opposite a busted partner it might fall one or two tricks short of making even three hearts. But it will be much easier to reach a makeable slam when partner holds a fair hand if you open with a two-bid.

Another method that both extends the use and sharpens the accuracy of opening strength-showing bids is to use a bidding system known as the artificial two-club bid. In this convention, two diamonds is used as the response showing weakness. In standard bidding, for example, there is an awkward no-man's-land that is far too wide between the 16-18 one-notrump opening and the 22–24-point two-notrump opening. This gray area is supposed to be handled by an opening bid of one in a suit, followed by a jump in notrump after partner responds, but this system of bidding still leaves too much guesswork for some players.

By playing the artificial two-club opening bid, you close the gap. In this system, an opening two-club bid followed by a two-notrump rebid shows 22-23; an opening three-notrump bid shows 24-25; an opening two-club bid followed by a three-notrump rebid shows 26-28. Thus 20-21 pointers may be opened two notrump.

Another virtue of the two-club opening is that it frees the other two-bids for other uses. Some use them for weak two-bids, on hands of less than opening-bid strength but with strong suits that will take about six tricks. Others use the two-club bid as game-forcing and the other two-bids to show strong hands of near-game strength but which nevertheless require a little bit of help.

Both systems work, but with unpracticed partnerships I suggest that you stick to the regular strong two-bid, or agree that two clubs is game-forcing and other two-bids are strong but demand only one "keep-the-bidding-open" response. However you may decide, it is wise to have a stated example hand as your minimum:

♠ **A K Q 9 7**   ♡ **A K J 9 8**   ◇ **3 2**   ♣ **2**

Some players would consider this hand worth a strong two-bid, and any player would welcome the chance to make an intermediate two-bid. This would avoid the disaster of playing at one spade when partner's bust includes a singleton spade when there's an easy game in hearts with nothing more than four or five trumps in his hand.

Responding to power bids   Once the two-bidder's partner has agreed to respect the obligation to respond on anything, he has no problem with a weak hand. There are, however, differing opinions as to the strength needed for a *positive* response. The more daring "standard" players argue that you should avoid a negative response on any hand with which you would have responded to an opening one-bid: i.e., 6 points or more, and should give the negative two-notrump response only with 0-5 points.

However, points alone do not appear to me to be the determining factor. To make a positive response of two hearts or two spades to an opening two-diamond bid on as few as six points *you need to have just about all those points in a good five-card suit.* With a four-card suit headed by the king-jack and a side queen, you are better advised to make your first bid conservative and carry on to game later.

More conservative players demand 1½ quick tricks* for a positive response. While I consider this a little stringent, I think it better than to make a positive response with a doubtful hand.

Again, any method that you and your partner agree upon is playable; the important thing is to have a precise agreement and stick to it.

For the benefit of those who know only point-count valuation, see page 204.
see page 204.

How do you respond with a weak hand to part-ner's opening bid?   The rule is: be brief. The first re-sponse by opener's partner is just about as important as the opening bid itself. It will seldom be possible to recover from a hasty first response, particularly when responder's hand is weak.

If you have a medium or strong hand—11 points and up—fac-ing partner's opening bid, it usually is not too difficult to reach a reasonably correct contract; you have the wherewithal to make two or more bids. But on weak hands of 6 to 10 points, it is seldom advisable to make more than one voluntary bid. It is particularly important to choose with great care the single bid that will give partner the best possible picture of your relative strength and distribution.

I am not sure I know exactly what feminine mystique is, but if it covers this kind of situation it finds women with an advan-tage and at the same time at a disadvantage. It isn't easy for us to accept the need for brevity; we naturally prefer to have a chatty discussion that describes the individual symptoms in some detail rather than say it all in a single word. On the other hand, we are accustomed to making a limited amount of wherewithal do the essential job. It becomes easy if we view an auction as just exactly that. Having come to the auction sale with only a limited amount of assets, it is essential for us to bid only on the item we can afford.

What too often happens is that instead of rationing ourselves to just one well-directed bid, we make a thoughtless first bid; then, on the next round, we realize we have not said exactly what we wanted to say, so we indulge in the extravagance of a second bid and find that we've said too much. Here's what can happen when you hold:

♠ A 8 7 3   ♡ Q 10 8   ◇ 5 2   ♣ 7 6 4 3

and partner opens with one heart. In spendthrift mood we decide to bid one spade. Opener's next bid is one notrump and we reflect that it's almost disloyal to conceal our support for partner's heart suit so we bid two hearts. By making two voluntary bids on a weak hand, we have dangerously overstated our strength and our partnership is quite likely to go overboard and bid game.

The proper procedure, of course, is to raise to two hearts on the first round. Since we can make only one bid, it is more important to show support for partner's suit and at the same time limit the strength we can hold. Partner knows that a raise shows from 7 to 9 or—at the most—10 points, and we've told our story.

There is a certain type of competitive auction that is mishandled in costly fashion by the "I'd rather make two bids than one" kind of partner. Holding a 6–10-point hand, she must choose between a simple raise of partner's suit or a one-over-one response in her own suit. South's hand is:

♠ K 9 7 2   ♡ 8 7 3   ◇ K J 3 2   ♣ J 8

North bid a diamond, East bid a heart and "of course" South bid one spade. Wrong! It is much better to bid two diamonds immediately, because this says that your hand is not strong—10 points at most. Later you may be lucky enough to get a chance to bid your own suit as well—but without claiming additional strength. For example:

NORTH	EAST	SOUTH	WEST
1 ◇	1 ♡	2 ◇	2 ♡
pass	pass	2 ♠	

Partner won't believe that you have suddenly discovered a hidden ace with this bid. You have limited your hand with your first bid. Now it is obvious you are merely making a competitive bid. But if you had bid one spade the first time and now were to come in

with a raise to three diamonds, partner would be right to expect
you to hold as much as 12-13 points.

Bid bold on big hands There are plenty of good responding bids to make with strong hands. The forcing double
raise, indicating 13 to 15 points, including distribution, is a fine
descriptive bid when you happen to hold immediate support for
opener's suit, and—on a different type of hand—a forcing two-notrump response, showing a balanced 13 to 15 high-card points,
is equally graphic. Nobody seems to have much trouble with these
two useful bids, but when it comes to the most powerful jump bid
in the book, there seems to be some doubt and confusion. I mean,
of course, the jump shift.

The main reason for confusion is a tendency in ultra-cautious
circles to jack up the point count needed for a jump shift. Thus,
although this bid was invented solely as a game-forcing maneuver
to show 17 points up, the idea has got around that it is risky to
employ it on less than about 19 or 20 points. And one school of
thought goes even farther and demands a strong fit in opener's
suit as well. Among such players, the jump shift is almost forcing
all the way to slam instead of merely to game, and is in danger of
becoming as rare as the whooping crane.

Unfortunately, this vogue for conservatism happens to tie in
with a notable feminine trait: women can be somewhat averse to
making expensive-sounding jump bids when they figure that a
"cheap" non-jump bid will do just as well. Which is a pity, because
quite often the cheap non-jump bid isn't cheap at all. Example:

NORTH	SOUTH
1 ♡	1 ♠
2 ♡	?

south holds: ♠ A Q J 6 5 3   ♡ 9 4   ◇ A J 10   ♣ K 2

A simple bid of two spades at this point would not be forcing and South dare not risk stopping short of game. She therefore has to bid *three* spades—which lifts the bidding to exactly the same level as if South had made a jump shift on the first round and followed with a simple spade rebid on the second round.

Here is another situation where a bold jump shift is in reality a much safer bid than a simple takeout:

NORTH	SOUTH
1 ♠	?

south holds: ♠ A Q 3 2   ♡ 10 5   ◇ A K Q 6 4   ♣ 8 6

If South jumps immediately to three diamonds, she can support spades on the next round and then relax. Having told the full story of her hand, she can leave further action to her partner.

Contrast this with what can happen if South bids only *two* diamonds on the first round. Over any rebid by North, South is too strong to raise merely to four spades, since slam may be there. But South is very badly situated to conduct a slam investigation, since she holds two losing cards in both hearts and clubs and has no good way to find out whether North can look after those suits. Thus a deal which could have been simple—had South forced the first time with a three-diamond bid—becomes a guessing contest.

Of course not every big hand is suitable for a jump-shift response. If you want to bid *two* suits without going beyond the three-notrump level, it can sometimes be better not to jump the bidding. Example:

NORTH	SOUTH
1 ♠	?

south holds: ♠ J 4   ♡ J 5 2   ◇ A Q J 7   ♣ A K J 3

If South's first bid is three diamonds or three clubs, she will be unable to show her other suit on the next round without ascending to the four-level. Therefore she should bid just *two* diamonds on the first round, continuing with three clubs if North rebids two spades. Since a change of suit by the responder is forcing for one round, the three-club bid is perfectly safe and should encourage North to bid notrump provided she holds a guard in the unbid heart suit.

Slam Bidding

Slams rank with abstract art, parking problems and the younger generation as the great passion rousers of modern times. Missing one is bad enough; bidding one that you are not going to make is worse.

In contracts more picayune than those of six or seven, defeat can be accepted stoically; but when a slam contract goes sour, the fact that someone has blundered is as unpalatable as it is inescapable. On the other hand, there's nothing quite like a *winning* slam.

Notrump slams are not a great problem. Everyone knows that 33 high-card points are needed for a small slam in notrump, and at least 37 to bid a grand slam. When either member of the team has bid notrump, it's pretty easy for the other member to figure out the team's total point count and to act accordingly. But when slam in a suit is under consideration, it isn't always easy for either player to gauge whether total assets in points and distribution top the magic 33-point mark. Consequently, some players never learn the knack of zeroing in on slam with tolerable accuracy.

The mistake most frequently made is to equate slam chances with the strength of the hand, when what really counts is *whether the hand is stronger than it might be*. This is the true test of whether you should go slam-hunting in any doubtful situation:

SOUTH	NORTH
1♠	2♣
2♡	4♡
?	

south holds: ♠ A K 5 3 2   ♡ K J 9 4   ◇ A 7   ♣ K 2

For all that North knows, South could hold a minimum opening—let's say the same hand without either the diamond ace or the club king. Those two cards represent two sure-fire tricks, so South has every reason to suppose she can win two tricks more than the minimum which North could expect. She should therefore launch into a Blackwood routine for a possible seven-bid and should bid six hearts even if an ace is missing.

More difficult are the situations where a player has only about one trick to spare, and therefore needs another extra trick from partner before slam can be bid. These situations are a stiff test of teamwork, but by asking yourself "Is my hand stronger than it might be?" you can usually gauge whether you ought to make a slam *suggestion* while leaving the final decision with your partner.

NORTH	SOUTH
1♠	2♡
4♡	?

south holds: ♠ K 3   ♡ A J 7 5 3 2   ◇ K 6 4   ♣ J 9

This is a pretty tough problem for South, but she holds several points more than the 10-point minimum needed for a two-level response to an opening bid. If North also holds a few points more than the 16 or so that would justify *her* previous bids, slam may be there. There is no sure way for South to find out, but she can put North in position to make an accurate decision by bidding five hearts. Any bid beyond the game level is a slam suggestion, so over five hearts it is North's turn to ask the familiar question, "Is my hand stronger than it might be?"

Notice that on the foregoing hand South could not solve her problem via the Blackwood Convention.* If, over a Blackwood four notrump, North responded five hearts to show two aces, South still would not know what to do. On a two-ace response to Blackwood, North might hold either of the following hands:

(a) ♠ A Q J 5 4   ♡ K Q 9 6   ◊ A 10 2   ♣ 4
(b) ♠ A Q J 6   ♡ K Q 10 4   ◊ A 7   ♣ 10 4 3

On (a), slam is laydown, but on (b), the opposition can cash two club tricks. The Blackwood Convention does not tell South which of these two hands North holds, but the recommended bid of five hearts allows North to take a partnership decision. On (b) North would pass five hearts while with (a) she would raise to six, because her hand not only is stronger than it might have been, it also includes first- or second-round control of the unbid suits and knowledge that the defenders can't collect two fast winners.

Paradoxically, it is on the very strongest hands that inexperienced slam-hunters tend to go astray. The bigger the hand, the more likely they are to overbid. Example:

SOUTH	NORTH
2 NT	3♠
3 NT	4♡
?	

south holds: ♠ Q 9 2   ♡ A K 5 4   ◊ K Q J   ♣ A K J

See Convention description, page 205.

South's 23-pointer has now been augmented by powerful support for hearts. Does South dare to conceal this great news from partner? Should she try for slam via Blackwood, or encourage with a bid of five hearts? The answer is that South should pass. The points have already been shown by the opening bid. The fine support for hearts is offset by the very skimpy support for spades, in which South does not hold anything remotely resembling a double-stopper; in fact, she doesn't even have a sure single-stopper. North must be off an ace and can hardly have enough strength in hearts and spades to make both those suits solid. In fact, there is absolutely no reason why North shouldn't hold even less than:

♠ K 7 6 5 4   ♡ Q J 9 6 2   ◇ 8   ♣ 10 3

Whatever you do after having bid a losing slam, don't pick that moment to discuss it with partner. With a regular partner, however, you might check back later on what bid put you on the losing track. The guilty bid will usually be the first one above the game level, and most often you'll discover that the player who made it did not ask the key question: "Is my hand stronger than it might be?"

Of Fears and Phobias

Do you suffer from partner-phobia—a morbid fear of facing an unfamiliar partner who has an unfamiliar style? If you do, you may be missing part of the pleasure that belongs with bridge, for this supremely social game can add an extra dimension to your relationships with people.

Actually, one should be more relaxed with high-powered partners than with others. The more expert a player is, the more she is to blame for any bloopers that are perpetrated by the team, because the chances are she could have done something to avoid them. My advice on how to handle partners who are more experienced than you is very simple: try hard, but never apologize.

By the same token, you have an extra responsibility when your partner is *less* experienced than you. Now you must bring all your resources of psychology and anticipation, as well as technical know-how, into play.

On playing with poorer partners   Experience shows that the final contract is usually decided *by the partner of the player* who first makes a bid that limits her strength. I don't suggest that you make a big production of this, but it will help if you can maneuver the bidding so that your partner limits her hand first. Therefore, don't strain to open with one notrump, which is a limit bid. Even though you play the cards better, partner's judgment of how high to go won't be as good as yours.

On the other hand, don't make the aggressive bid you would with an equal partner. For example, when you hold:

♠ J 7   ♡ K J 8 3   ♢ 10 8 2   ♣ K Q 5 3

and partner opens one spade, your hand justifies a two-club response. But I would bid a cautious one notrump so as to retain some control over future rounds of bidding. With a bit in reserve, I can take it from there if partner bids again. Notice, one notrump would not be "anti-system"; it is merely the cautious bid in a situation where there is a choice.

In rubber bridge, sacrifice contracts are not a wise investment if you figure your opponents are the stronger pair. You should be slightly less eager to open with a preemptive three-bid or to raise partner's three-spade bide to four with, for example:

♠ K 8 3   ♡ 7 3   ♢ J 10 7 6 4 2   ♣ J 8

No matter how good the "save," it's cheaper to lose the rubber.

Similarly, you should avoid borderline penalty doubles that could throw a strain on the team's defensive ability. It is a sound idea to decline to accept a very profitable double if you can make an easy game contract yourself and end the rubber. For example, with both sides vulnerable partner opens one spade, there is an overcall of two diamonds, and you hold:

♠ Q 3   ♡ K Q 9   ◇ A J 8 4   ♣ K J 9 7

With a regular partner you would double and expect to collect at least 800. But with an inexperienced partner it is better to settle for the game and rubber by bidding three notrump.

Bid boldly when you hold the spade suit.

♠ A 10 9 8 7 6   ♡ A J 10   ◇ 8 6   ♣ 8 2

It isn't a great opening bid, but with an inexperienced partner, don't dream of passing.

Bid so that, if possible, you get to play the difficult hands. You open with one notrump and partner, who has passed originally, jumps to three hearts. You might hold:

(a) ♠ K 10 3   ♡ A Q 3   ◇ K J 8 4   ♣ K J 6
(b) ♠ A 10 8   ♡ K Q 2   ◇ A 10 9 3   ♣ A J 9

With (a), bid three notrump, because the hand cannot be a lay-down at either three notrump or four hearts. But with (b), by all means bid four hearts and give your partner the pleasure of playing a hand that is likely to be cold.

There is a difference in approach on the next example. Your partner opens one notrump and you hold:

♠ A 2   ♡ 8 7 4   ◇ Q J 10 5 3 2   ♣ 8 4

Do you raise with a good partner, and sign off in diamonds with a beginner? My vote goes to a bold raise to three notrump with any partner. The success of this contract is apt to depend not so much on playing skill as on the cards partner holds in diamonds. If the contract fails, take the blame; if it makes, give partner the credit. Either way, you have made the right bid.

Bridge Behavior

Well, that's how to make your partnership work. My franchise was to stick to the bidding, but a player who is truly loyal can boost her team's winning chances in every phase of the game— even when she is dummy. I once witnessed an incident in a big American Contract Bridge League tournament where the North player gave an impressive exhibition of the art of how to score master points by refusing to score debating points.

```
                    ♠ A 9 8 7
                    ♡ K 4
                    ◇ K Q J 7
                    ♣ J 6 3
      ♠ 5          ┌──────────────┐      ♠ 10 6 3
      ♡ Q J 7 5 3 2│    NORTH      │      ♡ A 6
      ◇ 8 4 3      │ WEST     EAST │      ◇ A 10 6 5
      ♣ Q 10 4     │    SOUTH      │      ♣ 8 7 5 2
                   └──────────────┘
                    ♠ K Q J 4 2
                    ♡ 10 9 8
                    ◇ 9 2
                    ♣ A K 9
```

SOUTH	WEST	NORTH	EAST
1♠	pass	3♠	pass
4♠	pass	pass	pass

Against the four-spade contract, West opened the heart queen and South automatically slapped on dummy's king in order to build the ten into a third-round winner. East won the ace and fired back a heart for West to win—and when West played a third round of hearts South elected to ruff with dummy's nine of trumps. This was overruffed by East's tenspot. South had already lost three tricks and had to yield another to the diamond ace. Following is how the post mortem went, though you will appreciate that I can't reproduce *all* the inflections.

East said, "Too bad you didn't realize I could overruff the third round of hearts. If you go in with the ace of trumps instead of the nine, you can pull trumps and claim your contract after you have ditched a club loser on dummy's diamonds."

"I was *afraid* you might overruff the third heart lead," riposted South, "but it doesn't change anything if I ruff with the ace as you suggest. I would then have no reentry to dummy, and when you hold up the diamond ace for one round—as of course *you* would—I'd have no place to park my losing club. So you see, there was no way to win."

North was itching to get into the exchange but she bit her lip. After the tournament, she tactfully remarked that the contract could have been made by the unusual maneuver of not covering West's heart queen on the opening lead. This foregoes the chance of building a natural heart trick, but since a heart loser can be ruffed on the table anyway, that doesn't matter. And by not covering the first heart lead South prevents her opponents from leading the dangerous third round of hearts.

It was such an interesting solution to a tricky deal that few North players would have been strong-willed enough to refrain from saying so, even at the risk of upsetting partner. But by refusing to win the post mortem, North left her partner with morale to go on and win the tournament.

Quizzes

QUIZ 1 Both sides vulnerable, you are the dealer. What do you bid on each of the following hands?

1 ♠ Q 8 5 3   ♡ Q 8 6   ♢ A 7 6 4   ♣ K J
2 ♠ 7 6   ♡ K Q 9 2   ♢ A K 5 2   ♣ 8 6 3
3 ♠ 7   ♡ K J 10 9 7 4 2   ♢ A Q   ♣ 10 9 2
4 ♠ A K 10   ♡ A Q   ♢ K J 8 5 3   ♣ K Q J
5 ♠ J 5   ♡ A Q 9 7   ♢ A Q 4   ♣ K 7 4 3

Answers

1 *Pass*. It could be dangerous to open one spade, since the spade suit is not properly biddable and, if one diamond is opened, a two-club response would leave dealer with no satisfactory rebid. Since it is not obligatory to open on 13 points, it is better to pass and avoid headaches.

2 *One heart*. There are never any rebid problems when you are fortunate enough to hold two touching biddable suits; after opening the higher-ranking suit you can rebid the lower one at the cheapest level. And because all the high-card points are in the two biddable suits—a plus factor on *any* hand—the opening bid is recommended even though the point count is minimal.

3 *One heart*. Three hearts would be the bid if we were in third position, but a preemptive opening in first or second position *should not contain more than half a defensive trick outside the long suit*. A three-heart bid on this hand would make it impossible for partner to gauge defense prospects and would tend to erode partnership confidence.

4 *Two notrump*. The hand is one point short for a two-diamond opening, since a two-bid based on a five-card suit should contain

25 points. It is inadvisable to devalue these requirements, especially when an eminently correct two-notrump opening is available instead.

5 *One notrump.* There is no spade stop, but it is sound tactics to open notrump on any balanced 16–18-point hand that contains only one flaw.

QUIZ 2 Both sides vulnerable, your partner deals and opens one diamond. What do you call on each of the following hands?

1 ♠ 6 2 ♡ K 8 7 3 ◇ K 10 2 ♣ 9 6 4 3
2 ♠ Q 10 3 ♡ J 8 6 5 ◇ 10 5 ♣ K J 7 6
3 ♠ A K Q 8 4 ♡ A K J 4 2 ◇ 6 ♣ J 10
4 ♠ A Q ♡ A Q 3 ◇ 10 5 ♣ K J 9 7 6 5
5 ♠ 8 3 ♡ A K ◇ A Q J 8 ♣ Q J 5 3 2

Answers

1 *Two diamonds.* If you bid one heart and North rebids one spade or one notrump, you will convert to two diamonds. It is therefore better to support diamonds at once, thus making it abundantly clear that you hold a limited number of points. If you can make a heart game, opener will have to be so strong that she can bid two hearts over your two-diamond bid.

2 *One notrump.* On a 6–10-point hand that is worth only one bid, it is important to flash partner the briefest and best picture of the hand with that bid. Clearly a one-notrump response gives a better description of the hand than does a response of one heart.

3 *Two spades.* Don't be nervous about this jump shift with a singleton in opener's suit. The bid is forcing only to game, not to slam, and furthermore it doesn't cost any bidding space. If you bid only *one* spade you will have to jump to three hearts over opener's probable two-diamond rebid.

4 *Two clubs.* The hand and your trump suit are both slightly substandard for a jump shift. Chances are this deal belongs in three notrump with you as declarer, thus protecting your major-suit holdings against the opening lead. By bidding two clubs, the risk of the bidding zooming above the three-notrump level is reduced.

5 *Three clubs.* It is rarely wise to jump shift in such a weak suit but it can be quite a good move when you happen to hold very strong support for *opener's* suit. If opener happens to hold the top cards in clubs, she will realize that you hold the top diamonds, since you would not have forced on a weak suit unless you held compensating strength in partner's suit. Inferences of this type are sometimes the only way to reach slam.

QUIZ 3   In the following auctions, South has to decide whether the hand is worth a slam effort. With both sides vulnerable, what should South bid?

south holds:		NORTH	SOUTH
1 ♠ K 9 5 3 2		1 ♢	1 ♠
♡ 10		4 ♠	?
♢ K 9			
♣ K J 6 4 3			

		SOUTH	NORTH
2 ♠ A K		1 ♣	1 ♢
♡ A Q 10 5		2 ♡	3 ♡
♢ J 3		3NT	4 ♡
♣ A Q J 8 2		?	

		NORTH	SOUTH
3 ♠ 10 9		1 ♠	2 ♣
♡ J 10 8 3		3 ♡	?
♢ A 2			
♣ A Q 7 6 2			

south holds:

4   ♠ 7 3

    ♡ 10 8 3

    ♢ K 10 4 2

    ♣ K 9 8 6

NORTH	SOUTH
2 ♡	2NT
4 ♡	?

5   ♠ Q 5

    ♡ Q 2

    ♢ K Q J 9 8

    ♣ K Q J 5

NORTH	SOUTH
1 ♠	2 ♢
2 ♡	3NT
4 ♠	?

Answers

1 *Four notrump*. South needs only three aces in North's hand to make six spades a good bet. Asking herself the familiar slam question ("Is my hand stronger than it might be?") South notices that, although she has only about a king to spare for her one-spade response, she also holds a fifth spade when she might only hold four, and she controls the second round of both unbid suits. Furthermore, the diamond king is not just *any* old king but is a super-value "filler" for North's long diamond suit.

2 *Pass*. South holds a very fine hand indeed—but she has already apprised her partner of this fact and North is evidently not interested in slam. Holding nothing in reserve over her previous bids, South should respect partner's decision.

3 *Four notrump*. South holds three points more than the minimum of 10 points that are needed for a two-level response to an opening bid. Even more important is the fact that none of South's points is likely to be wasted, which means the hand will play above its face value. If South simply raises to four hearts, North will almost certainly pass, so it behooves South to take the initiative. (Four diamonds is also an acceptable move toward slam.)

4 *Five hearts*. A classic illustration of the proposition that what counts in slam bidding is not how strong your hand is but how

much you have in reserve from your previous bids. South has not yet promised a single point or a single trump, yet she holds very nearly enough for a positive response to the opening two-bid.

Notice that the recommended five-heart bid, in addition to telling North that South holds a near-positive response, also tells her South holds no aces. If South held an ace, she would cue-bid that suit instead of raising five hearts.

5 *Pass*. South has a few points to spare, but they are mainly in the minor suits and the signs are that the N-S hands do not combine well.

Rixi Markus

More international titles than any other woman in bridge

Rixi Markus has won more international championships than any other woman who has ever played bridge. She holds six European Woman's Bridge Team championships and three world crowns: the Women's Pair Olympiad, the Women's Team Olympiad, and the Mixed Team Olympiad. No player in all bridge history has won so many titles with so many different partners.

Scorers of the 1962 Pairs Olympiad used an electric computer. Within hours, the computer had a nickname: Rixi. The reason, obvious to any "in" player: there is no faster, surer player of the cards than Rixi Markus.

Rixi learned bridge in the gay Vienna of her girlhood, which produced so many of the world's great players. She was already a prodigy when Britain became her home before World War II. She speedily annexed every British championship and is the only woman bridge editor of a British daily. Her entertaining newspaper column on the game appears regularly in the famous *Manchester Guardian*.

Rixi is a bold bidder. A cynic (male, of course) once defined a chance remark as anything a man manages to say when two women are talking. Rixi's theme, however, is that in terms of competitive bidding, women don't talk enough. Her brilliant chapter on the subject of overcalls, though addressed to women, is to be read with profit by any bridge player—female or male.

The Art of the Overcall

Competitive bidding—women do not bid enough, men bid too much; both lose points ... by Rixi Markus

Even if a person talks a lot, it doesn't mean he or she talks too much. The days are long gone when polite silence could be counted a social asset. And nowhere is the knack of timely talk more valuable than through the medium of bridge bids.

Yet at the bridge table some women fail to talk enough with their bids. More points can be won by timely—and even by tiny—overcalls than in any other way. Women tend to miss these chances. Too often we sit on the sidelines, allowing our opponents to bid smoothly to the best spot.

Being a Winning Player

Although good overcalling is a large part of being a winning player, the secret lies in the timing. Knowing *when* to overcall counts more than anything else.

There are two kinds of overcalls: the crystal-clear "standard" bids that nobody should miss, and the more rewarding "optional" bids where judgment and flair lead one player to overcall while another player remains silent.

When to make a standard overcall   When your right-hand opponent opens one of a suit, you should seek a way to enter the auction if you hold the values for an opening bid: that is, at least 13 points, including distribution.

Because there just aren't enough bids available to handle all the card combinations you can hold, you will sometimes look in vain for an overcall that goes with your hand; most of the time you will have no trouble if you follow this six-point plan:

1 *Your hand contains a six-card or good five-card suit* With such a suit, you may overcall at either the one-level or the two-level, according to need. Example:

♠ K 5   ♡ Q 10 7 6 5 3   ◇ A K J   ♣ 6 3

If your opponent opens one club or one diamond, you have a safe bid of one heart. Even if the opening bid is one spade, you should venture two hearts, though the two-level overcall contains danger.

When you make a simple—i.e., a non-jump—overcall, you shouldn't hold *too many* points; 16 is normally the maximum. With 17 points up, you have to look for a stronger bid—either a takeout double (see later) or a jump overcall. A jump overcall usually shows a one-suited hand containing a strong six-carder or better. *It is not forcing.* The following hand rates a jump bid of two hearts after an opponent has opened one club or one diamond:

♠ 6 3   ♡ A K J 7 6 4   ◇ J 7   ♣ A Q 2

Even though a jump overcall is a strong bid,* it has a top

Editor's Note: Mrs. Markus, like most English players and many Americans, plays the jump overcall as showing an intermediate to strongish hand. Many experts employ a weak jump overcall as a preemptive tactic. We agree with Mrs. Markus that, against reasonably skilled opponents, this paper tiger advertises its own weakness and thereby loses much of its effect. Many players who use jump overcalls with good hands employ the bid not only on hands with one long, strong suit, but with strong two-suiters. It seems to this editor that a double is the better call for most strong hands that enjoy two suits worth bidding.

limit—around 19-21 points, according to vulnerability. On more powerful hands it is better to double. A jump overcall in a minor suit is often used as an invitation to three notrump.

2 *Your hand contains a strong four-card suit*   With this holding it is permissible to bid at the one-level but not at the two-level, since there is considerable risk of being doubled. Example:

♠ A K   ♡ 6 5 2   ◊ K Q J 8   ♣ 7 6 4 2

Over a one-club opening, you should enter the fray with a bid of one diamond. Over a heart or a spade opening, however, the pass is the only safe call. You should not bid the four-card diamond suit at the level of two.

Remember: it is even more important not to hold *too many* points than to hold too few. Partner will not expect more than 16 points, so if you keep any up your sleeve you run the risk of missing game.

3 *Your hand contains support for all the unbid suits*   With this type of hand you are very favorably situated, since you can double for takeout. Example:

♠ K J 8 3   ♡ 5   ◊ A Q 8 7   ♣ K 10 9 2

When your right-hand opponent opens one heart, you are in the enjoyable position of holding support for all the unbid suits and you can tell partner so by doubling for takeout. Do not be tempted to make a "cheap" overcall of one spade on this hand—although the one-spade bid may *look* cheap, it is poor value compared with the double, which shows three suits at once.

The takeout double was originally designed just to coax a bid out of partner when you could support all the unbid suits; but the double proved such an effective tool that it has been given added jobs. In addition to the I-can-support-anything-you-bid type of hand, it is now the fashion to double on practically every hand that is too strong for a simple suit overcall—any hand that contains 17 points up. The only exceptions to this rule are the hands that are suitable for a notrump overcall or a jump overcall.

The modern takeout double is probably the most important single tool in a bridge-player's survival kit. It therefore merits a specially close study (page 61).

4 *Your hand contains strength in the suit your opponent has opened* With 13 to 15 points, it is usually wise to keep quiet on the first round when you hold strength in the suit which has been bid against you. After you have passed the first round, you can change your mind and back in if the bidding fizzles out at a low level. Example:

♠ K J 10 2   ♡ J 7 5 2   ◇ A K Q   ♣ 5 2

If your opponent opens one spade, you should quietly pass and await developments. If perchance the next player bids hearts, you'll be mighty glad you kept quiet, since it is now dollars to doughnuts that there was no good spot for your side to play in. If, however, there is a one-notrump response on your left and this comes round to you, you can trot out a double, and hope partner can leave it in.

With a slightly stronger balanced hand containing strength in the enemy suit—16 to 18 points—the odds cease to favor an ambush; now the chance to win game yourself becomes a more dominant factor than the chance to set the opponents. The recommended maneuver is to overcall immediately with a bid of one notrump; this notrump overcall can even be the winning bid on a hand that would normally be unsuitable for a notrump *opening*. Example:

♠ A Q 8 3   ♡ K 7   ◇ A J 5 3 2   ♣ A 10

The only correct opening is one diamond. But if your right-hand opponent opens with a bid of one spade, the situation changes, because you no longer have time to describe your hand delicately by bidding diamonds followed by spades. Furthermore, the hand is too strong for a simple overcall and you do not have a strong enough suit for a jump overcall, and you certainly do not wish to encourage partner to bid hearts, via a takeout double. By far the best move you can make is to bid one notrump. In response, partner should bid in very much the same way as if you had opened notrump—except that your failure to double implies no great wish to hear a bid in the other major, hearts.

5 *Your hand contains a seven-card suit or better*   Freak hands built around long suits are a law unto themselves. On such hands, you must cast off those comfortable old point-count chains and rely upon plain common sense; the power of freak hands is not well expressed in point count.

First I would urge you to memorize an elementary proposition: *the object of bridge is to win games.* Too many players lose sight of this seemingly obvious fact. Example:

(a) ♠ A   ♡ K Q 10 9 7 4 2   ◇ Q 10 9 2   ♣ 2
(b) ♠ Q   ♡ A K J 8 7 5 3   ◇ A K 10   ♣ A 5

After an opening bid of one club on my right, I would jump to four hearts on both these hands, despite the widely-differing point count. Moreover, I would favor such action at any vulnerability situation. Theorists—usually male—argue that it is wrong to make similar bids on hands of different strength, but I am unrepentant; I am in business to win games, not to uphold theoretical principles.

On both hands there is a fair chance to make game and, after an enemy opening bid, I am willing to give up any chance to make slam. Nothing bad can happen if you jump to four hearts—but lots of bad things can happen if you stop to pick daisies. Example:

the opponents may locate a cheap save in spades.

The principle, then, is simple: if you hold a seven-card suit or better and are in nudging distance of game, bid it, don't waste time in small talk. You probably won't have much difficulty following this advice; I have noticed that women have a more realistic approach to these situations than men. But my next piece of advice is more controversial, since to some extent the recommended tactics run contrary to a woman's thrifty nature.

Thus far we have considered only *constructive* overcalls on hands where we have some chance to buy the contract—and make it. But it can be very good business to make a *preemptive* overcall even with very few points when holding a seven-card suit or better. Example:

♠ K Q 10 8 6 5 3 ♡ 8 ◇ J 5 ♣ 9 7 3

You should bid three spades over your opponent's opening bid of one club, one diamond or one heart. Although you do not expect to bring home this contract, the chances are you will be making a profitable trade if you are set. With one or more spades—or at favorable vulnerability—I would even bid *four* spades. In essence, you should overcall preemptively the same way as you open preemptively.

It is not an uncommon feminine failing to sidestep the challenge of these weak, long-suited hands. Some of us are averse to high-level bids that are likely to be defeated—probably because it offends our good-housekeeping instincts. For this reason, some women would prefer a bargain-price overcall of *one* spade on the example hand. If you suggest to such a player that she should leap to three spades, she will draw attention to the shortage of high-card points, but this of course is the very reason why she *should* bid high. Preemptive overcalls deny possession of high-card strength at the same time as they guarantee playing strength.

On the example hand the "cheap" overcall of *one* spade is a very poor buy compared with the "expensive" three-spade bid, since one spade fails to capitalize your chance to rob the opponents of several precious rounds of bidding; it also misleads partner into thinking you hold a fair slice of high-card points.

So, don't look for cheap buys when you hold a preemptive-type hand. Be bold, not balky—and if you are doubled, console yourself with the thought that the more you lose the more you save. Chances are the opponents were on their way to game or slam.

6 *Your hand contains game-going strength*   The majority of competitive auctions are nip-and-tuck contests, with both teams having a chance to buy the hand. Just occasionally, however, you will pick up a hand so big that even though your opponents have opened the bidding you are able to issue a game-going prospectus. This glad news can be handed to your partner by the simple expedient of cue-bidding the suit your opponents have opened. Suppose your right-hand opponent bids one club and you hold:

♠ J 8 5 3 ♡ A K J ◇ A K J 2 ♣ A J

Since you are prepared to contract for game, you should immediately overcall two clubs—the opponents' suit. This is simply a way to buy time to explore all the possible game contracts—four hearts, three notrump, or even five diamonds.

Partner is expected to keep the bidding open until game is reached, no matter how weak she may be. There is only one exception: she can drop the bidding in a situation like the following:

EAST	SOUTH	WEST	NORTH
1♣	2♣	pass	2♠
pass	3♠	pass	?

With a completely worthless hand, North is allowed to pass three spades. The reason for this escape clause is that if South can guarantee game opposite a Yarborough there is nothing to stop her bidding *four* spades instead of only three. The escape clause operates *only* when the responder holds a complete bust *and is raised short of game.*

Don't lose too much sleep over this situation; it won't often happen. More important, don't bid the opponents' suit just to see the wheels go round. If you hold a strong enough suit, it can pay better to settle for a direct game bid instead of opening the door to a conversation the enemy may be eager to join.

Such, then, are the ground rules for "standard" overcalls— and these rules should be at your fingertips. No matter how skilled you may be in other departments, you cannot afford to lose out on bread-and-butter bids.

If you vow to bid only in standard situations, your errors will never be big ones; but neither will your successes.

In a keen game, standard overcalls do not provide fat profits. They merely shut out losses. To make profits you have to be skilled in the art of "optional" overcalls, which means you must stake out a high percentage of winning decisions on problem hands—hands where one player might elect to overcall while a different player might not. These situations really count.

I could, I suppose, tag the ingredients of an "optional" over-call—points, hand pattern, vulnerability, and so on—rather like the ingredients of a cake mix, but I believe that is too slow an approach. A swifter—and, for women, a surer—definition of an optional overcall is: "A hand with too few points for a standard overcall, but on which you nevertheless feel a strong urge to splurge." Example:

(a) ♠ 5 3   ♡ K Q 10 5 4   ◇ K 8 6   ♣ 9 8 2
(b) ♠ J 10 3   ♡ Q 9 7   ◇ Q 8 7 3 2   ♣ K 5

Both hands contain 9 points—four fewer than are needed for a standard overcall—and both are 5-3-3-2 pattern. But there is a difference. On hand (a), when an opponent opens one club or one diamond, a bright player *wants* to overcall one heart. Such an overcall is by no means idle chatter—it may promote a good opening lead, or provide a springboard from which your team can contest a partial. Whenever an experienced player feels that kind of impulse, she's got an optional overcall.

On hand (b), by contrast, one feels no urge to act. The hand is featureless and monotonous and it is not sensible to indulge in purposeless activity that could help only the opponents.

Sophisticated sense   Once alerted to the possibility of an optional overcall, you need a sophisticated sense to reach an accurate and speedy decision. (If you hesitate and pass, you thereby give free information to keen-eared opponents.) A "Yes" answer to one or more of the following three questions should tend to influence you in favor of taking action.

1 *Is there a fair chance we can buy the hand?*   This test can slash away a large number of problems. It can save you from tripping into the trap that snares the player who blithely enters the auction on hands which offer no chance to buy, and who therefore merely helps the declarer to place the cards. Example:

♠ A 5   ♡ 6 2   ◇ K J 7   ♣ K 10 7 6 5 3

If your partner deals and passes and your opponent opens one spade, there is very little purpose in bidding two clubs. Since your partner failed to open the bidding, the opponents probably own the majority of points, as well as the key spade suit. But if your *opponent* dealt and opened one spade there would be a better argument in favor of bidding two clubs, since partner has not yet passed and there is some chance the hand belongs to your team.

The two-club overcall would still be risky, but it would not be surely futile. The moral is that you have a better chance to buy the hand if your partner has not already passed.

Possession of the spade suit is a key factor in assessing your chance to buy the hand. Example:

♠ 8   ♡ J 10 9 2   ◇ K J 8 6   ♣ A Q 10 2

After a pass from partner and a one-spade bid on my right I would not double for takeout. Even if my partner held a biddable club, diamond or heart suit it is unlikely we could profitably outbid the opponents' spade suit. To double, therefore, would merely betray my hand to the declarer. But suppose my right-hand opponent opened one *heart* and my heart and spade holdings were reversed. I would venture a takeout double, since the chance of finding a spade fit in partner's hand would vastly improve our chances of securing the contract at an economic level.

2   *Do I want my suit led?*   Most women will cheerfully allow differences of opinion over bidding and card play, but they will allow little leeway on the opening lead. If they've bid a suit, they rightly expect partner to lead it.

But just *because* partner will nearly always open the suit you have bid, *you are obligated not to overcall in a bad suit.* Imagine partner's feelings when she loyally leads, say the king from K x, only to find that you have overcalled with J x x x! This means that, on a close decision, you should not make an optional overcall in a suit you don't want led. Conversely, with a strong enough suit, it *can* be good tactics to overcall for the sole purpose of promoting a lead. Example:

(a) ♠ 5   ♡ 9 8 7 2   ◇ A K J 10 5   ♣ 8 7 4
(b) ♠ K 2   ♡ K 10 5   ◇ J 8 6 5 3   ♣ K 6 2

After partner has passed, there is a one-club opening on your right. On hand (a) you have no chance to buy the contract, yet it is a bright idea to bid one diamond, since a lead of this suit will be best against any enemy contract. On hand (b), however, it would be wrong to overcall one diamond; a diamond opening is unlikely to be best unless partner leads that suit of her own free will, and you are fortunate enough to possess a key card in any other suit that she may elect to open.

3 *Can I steal space?*   This third test of an optional overcall is most important—yet the "space" concept of overcalling is virtually a new frontier. If you can get a grasp of this concept, you will be able to overcall more profitably than many long-time experts.

   I can dramatize the space concept by recalling a deal that helped my team win a tournament:

```
                        ♠ Q 10 9 4
                        ♡ A 8
                        ◇ A K 8 3 2
                        ♣ J 5
    ♠ 7 6 5          ┌──────────────────┐   ♠ A 8
    ♡ J 9 6 3        │     NORTH        │   ♡ Q 10 7 4
    ◇ J 7 5          │ WEST      EAST   │   ◇ 6 4
    ♣ A 6 3          │     SOUTH        │   ♣ K Q 9 8 7
                     └──────────────────┘
                        ♠ K J 3 2
                        ♡ K 5 2
                        ◇ Q 10 9
                        ♣ 10 4 2
```

With North-South vulnerable, the bidding at one table went as follows:

NORTH	EAST	SOUTH	WEST
1 ♢	1 ♡	1 ♠	2 ♡
2 ♠	pass	3 ♢	pass
4 ♠	pass	pass	pass

East's "cheap" one-heart overcall was an attempt to take advantage of the vulnerability situation. There was little danger in the overcall—but neither was there much prospect of profit. Brushing interference aside, North-South bid smoothly to the right spot. There were no problems in the play and the vulnerable four-spade contract was easily wrapped up.

Contrast this with events at the other table:

NORTH	EAST	SOUTH	WEST
1 ♢	2 ♣	2 ♢	pass
pass	pass		

Again East exploited the vulnerability situation to make a saucy overcall—but this time she chose the space-stealing bid of two clubs instead of the one-heart bid. Now South could not show spades cheaply and was not strong enough to bid the suit at the two-level; South therefore settled for the obvious two-diamond bid and the auction fizzled to a stop. North rightly figured that an 11-trick game in diamonds could not be made, and he did not have the powerful hand that a bid of two spades would promise in this situation.

The conclusion is obvious. The one-heart overcall did not discomfit South, since it did not shut out the spade suit; to put it another way, the one-heart overcall *did not steal bidding space.* But at the other table the two-club overcall was a killer, since it interfered with the normal flow of bidding; *it stole space.*

In calculating whether to make an optional overcall, therefore, one should be much more venturesome with overcalls that preempt enemy bidding space than with overcalls that do not. Can you supply the winning answers in the following "optional" situations?

With neither side vulnerable, your partner deals and passes. You hold:

(a) ♠ 8 7 5   ♡ K 2   ◇ A 6   ♣ K 10 9 7 4 3
Your opponent opens one diamond.

(b) ♠ 9 4 2   ♡ J 8 3   ◇ K 5   ♣ A Q 8 5 4
Your opponent opens one spade.

(c) ♠ Q 10 9 7 2   ♡ 7 5   ◇ K 9 3   ♣ K 8 2
Your opponent opens one club.

On (a) I would overcall two clubs, since this may shut out an enemy contract in one of the major suits. On hand (b) I favor the pass, since a two-club overcall does not toss even a midget-size monkey wrench into the opponents' bidding machinery. On hand (c) a nuisance bid of one spade is in order, since it may freeze out a heart bid.

Responding to a suit overcall   Many players find it extremely difficult to decide what is the proper response to partner's overcall—largely because they do not appreciate that the accent should be on simple and direct methods rather than on subtlety.

When your partner makes an overcall in a suit, you do not make the same response as if she had *opened* the bidding. This is because an overcall shows a humbler hand than an opening bid;

the point count can be as low as 8 or 9, and the top limit is 16. (Holding more than 16 points, you don't overcall; you double for takeout or make a *jump* overcall.) This 16-point top determines how many points are needed for a constructive response.

The responder's magic number is 10. Seldom can you make game on less, since partner will hold at most 16 of the 26 points that are needed for game. Therefore 10 points is the ante for a constructive raise of partner's suit, or for a minimum bid in notrump; while as many as 12 or 13 points are needed for a double raise, or for a jump bid in notrump. Suppose the bidding goes:

WEST	NORTH	EAST	SOUTH
1♣	1♠	pass	?

Both sides are vulnerable and South holds:

(a) ♠ 6 2   ♡ Q 10 8 5 2   ◇ A Q 7   ♣ 9 8 6
(b) ♠ Q 9 7   ♡ A 8 7 5   ◇ K 7 5 2   ♣ 8 6
(c) ♠ 8 3   ♡ K J 6   ◇ K J 8 2   ♣ Q J 9 2
(d) ♠ A 10 7   ♡ 9 8 6 5   ◇ A Q 8 5 3   ♣ 7

Hand (a) does not rate a bid, since South can add only 9 points to North's maximum of 16.

Hand (b) is worth a gentle boost to two spades, since it contains 10 points blended with trump support. Notice that it is quite in order to raise on three-card support; indeed, if partner overcalls at the two level—thus showing at least a five-card suit—you may raise on a doubleton honor if no better bid is available.

Hand (c) merits a takeout into one notrump, since if North is close to his 16-point maximum game may be there. Notice that one should bid notrump only if there is a chance to make game.

Hand (d) is worth a raise to *three* spades. Although it is seldom wise to jump an *opening* bid on three-card trump support, you need have no such inhibitions when raising an overcall, since overcalls are usually based on a long suit. Notice that you can't bid two diamonds as a curtain-raiser, since a new suit over an overcall is not forcing. If, on a stronger hand, you wanted to force in diamonds, you would have to jump to three.

A simple bid in a new suit shows a suit that may be safer to play in than the suit partner has bid. Example:

WEST	NORTH	EAST	SOUTH
1♣	1♠	pass	?

♠ 6   ♡ A Q 10 9 5 2   ◇ J 10 8   ♣ 8 5 4

It is proper to bid two hearts, since this may be a better spot than one spade. The two-heart bid does not necessarily invite North to bid again; without heart support plus a reasonable quota of fast tricks North will probably pass.

The above rules are designed for *constructive* bidding after partner has made an overcall in a suit. Follow them when you are vulnerable, and also when neither side is vulnerable. But at *favorable* vulnerability—that is, when the opponents are vulnerable and you are not—you can throw the 10-point rule overboard if you hold support for partner's suit. Example:

WEST	NORTH	EAST	SOUTH
1◇	1♠	pass	?

♠ J 8 5 3   ♡ K 9 7 6 2   ◇ 8 5   ♣ J 2

Though there is virtually no chance to make game, a raise to two spades is the move. A non-vulnerable raise of this type is not constructive but merely aims to freeze West out of the auction.

Partner may very well be set in two spades, but the arithmetic of the situation is solidly in your favor.

The overcaller must be cagey when her suit has been accorded a non-vulnerable raise. Suppose you are South, with E-W vulnerable:

EAST	SOUTH	WEST	NORTH
1♣	1♠	pass	2♠
pass	?		

♠ A K Q 8 4   ♡ J 4   ◇ K J 7   ♣ 10 4 3

Although South holds a maximum hand, she would be unwise to proceed straight to game; at the prevailing vulnerability, North may have scraped the barrel. South should therefore allow leeway by making a game-try bid. In this instance, a bid of three diamonds is the recommended maneuver; this enables North to jump to game if she holds a genuine hand, or to sign off in three spades if she is weak.

One last tip to sharpen the accuracy of your response to overcalls. If your partner makes an overcall that does *not* steal bidding space, she is more likely to hold a genuine standard overcall than a skinny optional overcall. You can turn this knowledge to advantage in a situation like the following:

WEST	NORTH	EAST	SOUTH
1◇	1♡	pass	?

♠ A 10 3   ♡ Q 9 6   ◇ J 10 8 3   ♣ A 10 8

Although South's heart support is adequate for a raise of North's suit, the balanced hand pattern and widely dispersed honor cards tend to favor a bid of notrump. However, having decided to bid notrump, South is faced with a knife-edge choice between bidding a cautious one notrump or a slightly extravagant two notrump. (South is a point shy for the two-notrump bid, but she holds three tens to compensate.) What would be your choice?

My vote goes in favor of *two* notrump. North's one-heart bid over one diamond was manifestly not made with the object of stealing space, so is likely to be based on a genuine hand. Game is therefore a real possibility.

Responding to a jump overcall

Although a jump over-call shows a strong one-suited hand, it is not forcing and it denies the strength to bid game. In the somewhat free-wheeling style that I favor, the bedrock minimum is 15 points, while 17-19 is ideal.

Before responding to a jump overcall, you should notice the vulnerability, as well as the level, at which the overcall was made. A vulnerable overcall of three clubs, for instance, is likely to be based on a stronger hand than a non-vulnerable overcall of two spades. Such considerations should influence your response. Example:

N-S vulnerable.

WEST	NORTH	EAST	SOUTH
1 ◇	3 ♣	pass	?

E-W vulnerable.

WEST	NORTH	EAST	SOUTH
1 ◇	2 ♠	pass	?

In each case South holds:

♠ J 8 4   ♡ Q J 5 3   ◇ Q J 7   ♣ J 8 2

In the first auction South should bid three notrump, since North is likely to be especially strong. At the prevailing vulnerability, a *two*-club overcall could show quite a nourishing hand, so the three-club bid can be as strong as:

♠ A 6   ♡ A 2   ◇ 5 4 3   ♣ A K Q 10 7 4

In the second auction South should pass, since North may have "stretched" to distinguish her hand from the motley collection on which she could overcall *one* spade at this special vulnerability. North's jump overcall could be based on this type of hand:

♠ A Q 10 9 7 3   ♡ 8 2   ◇ K 5   ♣ K Q 4

A new-suit response to a jump overcall is forcing. This is because a jump overcall always shows a strong suit, so there is no sense in the responder bidding a new suit except as a forward-going move to game. Example:

WEST	NORTH	EAST	SOUTH
1 ♡	3 ♣	pass	?

south holds: ♠ 10 9 7   ♡ 9 8 6 5   ◇ A K 10   ♣ K 8 6

South should bid three diamonds. This may seem a fancy bid, but it may be the only way to prod North into three notrump if she holds a heart guard. Since the three-diamond bid is forcing, it cannot go awry and South can always go back to clubs if the auction fails to develop as desired.

The takeout double
A takeout double is an invitation to partner; and you can be just as generous or tightfisted with this type of invitation as with any other kind. The frequency with

which you double for takeout is therefore a very revealing personality guide.

Like everyone but a nervous novice, you probably get a kick out of being declarer; but if you double for takeout instead of bidding a suit you are less likely to enjoy that privilege. This is because after a double the doubler's partner usually winds up playing the hand. Naturally, a well balanced player ignores this factor and bases her decision entirely on the merits of her hand.

But some selfish players never double if they can dredge up a suit overcall—not even if their hand contains support for all the unbid suits. They are prepared to risk reaching the wrong contract just so they can have the fun of being declarer. Fortunately, bridge is a game of near-perfect justice and such players are eventually brought down to earth by the pull of financial gravity.

Can you always distinguish a takeout double from a penalty double? To distinguish between the two types of doubles, remember this proposition: *A double is for takeout if it is made at the player's first opportunity of doubling, provided her partner has not made any bid.* That proposition supplies all the answers. Example:

WEST	NORTH	EAST	SOUTH
pass	pass	1♡	double

South's double is for takeout because it is made at the first opportunity and North has not bid.

WEST	NORTH	EAST	SOUTH
pass	1♣	1♠	double

South's double is not a takeout double because her partner has made a bid.

WEST	NORTH	EAST	SOUTH
pass	pass	1 ♠	pass
2 ♣	double		

This is the kind of bidding sequence that can cause misunderstanding. Although North's double is not made at the first opportunity of *bidding,* it is made at the first opportunity of *doubling.* The double is therefore for takeout.

WEST	NORTH	EAST	SOUTH
1 ♠	pass	1 NT	pass
2 ♠	double		

North's double is for penalty. Had she wanted to double for takeout she would have doubled the first time.

The takeout double is a way to tell partner you hold as good as an opening bid and that the deal may belong to your team even though the opponents have opened the bidding; but you must hold the right type of hand as well as holding at least 13 points.

When you ask partner to be your guest via a takeout double, you extend an open invitation, and you don't know at what bidding level she may accept, nor in what suit. Therefore, before you can double you must be sure you can handle everything that can happen. If you obey the "how to double" rules, you will find you *can* handle everything.

How to double on 13-16 points   This is the minimum point count for a takeout double, which means you need to hold a special three-suited hand pattern. Best is 4-4-4-1 or 5-4-4-0—the shortage, of course, being in the opponents' suit—and with such a pattern you can double even if you are rock bottom on points. Example:

♠ A Q 9 3   ♡ 6   ◇ J 10 8 2   ♣ K J 8 5

Even if you are vulnerable, this is a fine doubling hand after your opponent has opened one heart, since you hold strong support for the other three suits. Of course, if the opening bid were one *spade* instead of one heart, you would pass. Lacking support for the hearts, the suit your partner is most likely to respond in, a double would be suicidal.

Which brings us to an important point. In responding to a double, your partner will bid a major suit if she can. Therefore if you double a minor-suit opening you should preferably hold support for both major suits, while if you double a major-suit opening it is highly desirable that you should possess four-card support for the *unbid* major. Example:

♠ A 10 2   ♡ Q J 9   ◇ 8 3   ♣ A Q 5 4 2

Although not perfect, you can double an opening bid of one diamond on this hand, since partner will not go overboard on the assumption that you hold four cards in *both* major suits. The double is more evocative of all-round strength in the unbid suits than a two-club overcall.

Now suppose your opponent opens one heart instead of one diamond. This situation is very different, since if you double a major your partner expects you to deliver four-card support for the unbid major. She might therefore elect to bid a very weak four-card spade suit, with poor results. (This danger is in fact even more menacing than the apparent danger that partner might respond to a double of one heart by bidding diamonds, since it is good tactics to bid a four-card major suit in response to a double in preference to a strong minor suit.) Therefore I would not double a one-heart opening; I would either pass or bid two clubs, depending on such factors as the vulnerability situation and my estimate of the opposition's card-play ability.

As your point count climbs above the 13-point bedrock, you

can double even if there are small gaps in your coverage of the unbid suits. It is good tactics to double an opening bid of one spade on each of the following hands:

(a) ♠ 9 5   ♡ A K J 6   ♢ J 4 2   ♣ K Q 9 3
(b) ♠ 7 6 2   ♡ K Q 9 8   ♢ A K J 6   ♣ Q 2
(c) ♠ 8 4   ♡ K J 9   ♢ A Q 10 2   ♣ K Q J 7

On (a) the fact that you hold 15 points compensates for the poor quality of your diamond holding. Hand (b) is slightly unusual in that you hold three cards in the enemy suit and only a doubleton in one of the unbid suits; but these are relatively minor deficiencies and you do hold four cards in the unbid major suit. On hand (c) the lack of a fourth heart is a disadvantage but the hand is perfect in other respects and contains a high point-count; therefore the double is a risk that should be accepted.

How to double on 17 points up   When we held only 13-16 points, we could afford to double only if we held an acceptable hand-pattern. We had to be sure our slender resources were in the right places so we could cope with any response partner might make. But with 17 points up, we have remarkably few problems; those extra points are our survival kit and will take care of future developments, even if partner bids a suit we are short on. It is fortunate that this is so; for, as we have already seen, you cannot make a simple overcall on hands containing 17 points up, so we have to have a way to describe these hands.

Instead of worrying whether you can afford to double you can say to yourself, "I *know* I can double if I want to; but first let me see if there is any other bid that describes my hand better." Since a 17-point hand is too strong for a suit overcall, there are only two bids that might be better than a double—a notrump overcall or a jump overcall. Therefore, if you hold 17 points and your hand is not suitable for a notrump overcall or a jump overcall in a suit, you should "always" double. (I use quote marks only because there is no such thing as "always" or "never" in bridge.)

Following are some situations where your right-hand opponent opens the bidding and you hold a hand that is not suitable for notrump or for a jump bid. Therefore you have to double, even though your hand does not contain support for all the unbid suits. I will explain how to handle any awkward situations that may develop after the double.

♠ 2   ♡ A K J 6   ◇ K 10 8 6 4   ♣ A K 3

After you have doubled a one-club opening, your partner is unlikely to oblige by bidding a red suit; she is more likely to bid one spade. If this happens, you should convert to one notrump. Such a move has the advantage of showing a high point-count, since with a minimum double you would pass any non-forcing response from partner. Notice that if partner responds to your double by bidding spades *above* the one-level, the combined strength of the two hands will be such that you should easily make game somewhere.

♠ A K 6 3 2   ♡ A K 10 9 2   ◇ 5   ♣ K 8

The reason this hand is not suitable for a jump overcall after your opponent has opened one club is that you may pick the wrong suit—and since a jump overcall is not forcing, your partner may pass with a hand that could conceivably make game. It is therefore better to double and then bid spades over partner's expected diamond response; such a move leaves you in position to bid hearts if partner takes any further action.

♠ Q   ♡ Q 8 5 3   ◇ A K Q 10 9 2   ♣ A J

This time your opponent opens one spade. Now you can capitalize on the fact that a double of one major suit usually shows four-card support for the other major: by doubling instead of bidding three diamonds, you give your team a much better chance of reaching a heart game should partner hold a moderate four-card suit.

Notice that on the above hands you could double with the "wrong" hand-pattern only because you held extra points. With a minimum point-count the double would be inadvisable.

Responding to a takeout double Your partner's takeout double is an invitation to bid. This invitation you may refuse only at your peril. In fact, it is more like a royal command. No matter how short you are on points, you should respond to a double unless your right-hand opponent lets you off the hook by making a bid, in which case you can pass a weak hand.

The art of responding to a takeout double is different from the art of responding to an opening bid. The response to an opening bid is frequently just a preliminary gambit in quite a long conversation. But when you respond to a double, it is quite possible this will be your last chance to bid. Therefore your response has got to say something fast: you must search for the salient feature in your hand and convey it to your partner in a single bid.

First you have to decide whether your hand is weak, medium or strong. Weak hands are those containing 0-8 points, medium hands are 9-11, and strong hands are 12 points up. The winning responses with each type of hand are as follows:

Responder holds 0-8 points There is just one consolation in holding a bad hand. You have no headache figuring out what to bid. You simply bid a suit at the cheapest possible level. The only time you do not make the cheapest possible bid on a 0–8-point hand is when you hold two suits of equal length, one of which is a major and the other a minor; then you should usually bid the

major suit, since on the takeout double your partner is more likely
to hold four cards in that suit. Example:

WEST	NORTH	EAST	SOUTH
1 ♣	double	pass	?

south holds: (a) ♠ K 4   ♡ 8 7 5 3   ◇ 10 7 5 2   ♣ Q 5 3
           (b) ♠ 10 9 3 2   ♡ 8 4 3   ◇ 9 6   ♣ K J 9 2
           (c) ♠ 9 8 6   ♡ 10 7 2   ◇ K 2   ♣ 9 7 6 5 3

(a) Even on this uninspiring layout, it can make a difference which suit you bid. The one-heart response has a definite edge
over one diamond, because North is more likely to hold strength
in the major suits.

(b) Although South holds a guard in the suit West has
opened, one spade is a better response to North's double than one
notrump. One notrump is best used as a special response on hands
which contain around 7-10 points.

(c) At first glance this drab hand seems unbiddable, but
South should remember this is North's party and should dutifully
respond one heart on a three-card suit. One heart is not a fancy
bid; it is South's "best" and cheapest suit, and is therefore as
orthodox as a curate's first sermon.

If your opponent bids over the double, you do not have to
bid on a 0-8-point hand. But if you get a chance to show a suit
very cheaply, it can be good policy to bid even though you are not
compelled to.

WEST	NORTH	EAST	SOUTH
1 ♣	double	1 ♡	?

south holds: ♠ Q 9 7 3   ♡ 7 3   ◇ A 10 5   ♣ 8 5 4 3

A free bid of one spade is tactically better than a pass, other-wise North-South could get shut out of the auction by a one-notrump rebid from West. But if South's spades are changed with her diamonds, the same considerations do not arise: South can no longer show a suit at the level of one, and a pass is better than a free bid of two diamonds.

Rebids after an 0–8-point response   A minimum response can show a fairly wide range of points—a factor which does not aid precise bidding—but the doubling partners have two things going for them when they tackle the decision whether to settle for part-score or go for game. First, they know the location of most of their opponents' points and can judge whether their own points are "working"; second, since the doubler is known—or rather, is *expected*—to be short in the suit bid by the opponents, the doubler's partner can put a more-accurate-than-usual appraisal on any high cards held in that suit. Suppose the bidding goes like this:

WEST	NORTH	EAST	SOUTH
1 ♡	double	pass	1 ♠
pass	2 ♠	pass	?

south holds:
(a) ♠ K 8 3 2   ♡ K 7   ◇ J 10 6 5   ♣ 10 7 3
(b) ♠ K 7 5 4   ♡ 9 7 6 3   ◇ J 10 6   ♣ K 10
(c) ♠ Q 9 7 5   ♡ A 2   ◇ J 10 6   ♣ 10 7 3 2

Having shown 0-8 points by responding one spade, South can appraise matters more accurately on the second round of bidding. And although each of the above hands contains exactly the same number of points, South does not make the same call on each hand.

On hand (a) South should pass two spades because the dou-bleton heart king is likely to be useless. North is expected to be short in hearts on her takeout double, and West is likely to hold the heart ace.

On hand (b) by contrast, every point is working. South holds no wasted high cards in the enemy heart suit and North's expected heart shortage will take care of South's losers. Furthermore, South holds good cards in clubs and diamonds, where North is likely to need assistance. It would be hard to find a better 8-point hand for South. A raise to four spades is fair speculation.

Hand (c) is about average value. The heart ace is worth a trick, but it won't help build any extra winners in North's hand. It would help if South's short suit were in clubs or diamonds instead of in West's heart suit, where it may merely duplicate a heart shortage in North's hand. However, South would have had to bid one spade even if she held no points at all. So, with a sound partner, South is worth a raise to three spades.

The doubler, as well as the responder, has the chance to use fine judgment. On the following layout, both sides are vulnerable:

```
                    ♠ 9 6 4 2
                    ♡ Q 7 3 2
                    ◊ Q 10 8
                    ♣ K 2
                 ┌─────────────┐
♠ Q 7 3          │    NORTH    │         ♠ A K J 8 5
♡ 10 6 4         │             │         ♡ J 8
◊ 7 4 2          │ WEST   EAST │         ◊ K 6 3
♣ J 9 6 3        │             │         ♣ A 10 8
                 │    SOUTH    │
                 └─────────────┘
                    ♠ 10
                    ♡ A K 9 5
                    ◊ A J 9 5
                    ♣ Q 7 5 4
```

EAST	SOUTH	WEST	NORTH
1 ♠	double	pass	2 ♡
pass	3 ♡	pass	4 ♡
pass	pass	pass	

Holding 0-8 points, North made a minimum response.

South holds just 16 points—not normally enough for game, even if North holds her 8-point maximum—but she has a classic 4-4-4-1 hand pattern. Also, South knows that any missing high cards in diamonds and clubs are likely to be located in East's hands. This factor will probably enable the declarer to win more tricks than usual, so South raises to three hearts.

North is delighted to have a second chance to bid. Thus far, she has not shown any points at all, so her hand is far better than it might be; also, she holds no potentially wasted points in spades. North therefore bids game, and even though there are only 24 points in the combined hands North easily wraps up eleven tricks. Lucky? It is true the North-South hands fit like a Paris gown, and the diamond king is onside—but these are the reasons North-South bid game, even though they knew they were short on points. Had North-South held wasted points in the spade suit, and had *West* opened the bidding instead of East, they would have settled for partscore.

Responder holds 9-11 points   We have noticed that after a take-out double you may make game on less than the 26 points that are normally required. Therefore when the responder holds 9-11 points there is quite a big chance of landing game. The responder conveys this message to her partner by making a jump response. Example:

WEST	NORTH	EAST	SOUTH
1 ♡	double	pass	2 ♠

A minimum hand for South would be as follows:

♠ K J 8 2   ♡ 8 6 5   ◇ A J 6   ♣ 10 9 3

On that hand, the jump bid is a pretty close decision. Interchange the black suits so that South has four clubs and three spades, and the lack of a major suit would make it prudent to give a minimum response.

Good players sometimes bend the point-count rules. It is not impossible to jump on only an 8-point hand; conversely, it can be wise to make a minimum response on as many as 9 or 10 points. Possession of a major suit is always a vital factor in such calculations.

A jump response is highly encouraging but not forcing, not even for one round. (Hands which merit a forcing bid—12 points and upwards—are handled in a special way.) If your partner doubles a one-heart opening, the top hand for a jump response of two spades would be something like this (less than 12 points but containing a 5-card major):

♠ K 10 7 5 3   ♡ 9 8 2   ◇ K 5   ♣ A 10 9

If an opponent intervenes over your partner's double, you don't necessarily have to jump to show 9-11 points. When you are bidding over an opponent, *any* bid will show that your hand contains some strength.

WEST	NORTH	EAST	SOUTH
1♠	double	2♠	3◇

An average hand for South would be something like this:

♠ 8 5 4   ♡ Q 10 7   ◇ K J 8 5 3   ♣ K 6

Rebids after a 9–11-point response   If the team can locate a major-suit fit, there will usually be a game in the hand. If there is no major-suit fit and the doubler holds a minimum hand, she can pass the jump response.

EAST	SOUTH	WEST	NORTH
1♣	double	pass	2♠
pass	?		

south holds: (a) ♠ A Q 5 4   ♡ 6   ◇ A 10 8 3   ♣ K J 9 8

(b) ♠ K J 9   ♡ 9 5   ◇ K J 10 2   ♣ A 7 6 2

(c) ♠ Q 10 8 6   ♡ J 2   ◇ A K 5   ♣ A 9 7 3

(a) South holds better than minimum and she holds four-card support for the suit North has bid. Game should present no problems, so South raises directly to four spades. Even if South held a couple of points less in high cards, she would still be worth a single raise to three spades, since she holds a classic three-suited hand pattern.

(b) is a minimum double and it also contains a blemish, inasmuch as it lacks four-card spade support. Since North's two-spade bid is not forcing, South should pass.

(c) presents a tough decision. It contains a point or two more than the minimum, plus four-card spade support, but there are two losing cards in the opponents' suit. A raise to just three spades is the solution.

If the doubler holds plenty of points but is unsure of the best game spot, a forcing bid in the enemy suit will buy time for exploration.

EAST	SOUTH	WEST	NORTH
1◇	double	pass	2♠
pass	?		

south holds: ♠ Q 9 4   ♡ A K 8 7   ◇ Q 2   ♣ A K 10 6

There is only one good bid for South to make—a cue-bid in the enemy suit. The three-diamond bid does not say anything about

South's diamond holding; it merely says, "We can make game, but I'm not sure of the safest spot. Please rebid your suit, if it's rebid-dable, or bid another suit, or bid notrump."

The value of this cue-bid maneuver is obvious if you consider the alternatives. Three hearts would not be a good bid for South to make, since it suggests a five-card suit. Three spades is too weak a bid, since North might pass. Finally, a jump to four spades could be wrong if North held only a four-card spade suit. But by cue-bidding the enemy suit, South is sure to locate the best spot, be it notrump, hearts or spades.

Responder holds 12 points up   It is usually a fair gamble to contract for game if you hold 12 points opposite your partner's takeout double. With a strong suit you should jump to game.

WEST	NORTH	EAST	SOUTH
1 ♡	double	3 ♡	4 ♠

south could hold: ♠ K 9 8 6 4   ♡ 8 5 3   ◇ A J 9 2   ♣ Q

By doubling hearts for takeout, North promised to deliver support for spades (or an extra-strong hand). Therefore South is safe in jumping to game on an apparently spindly suit. The lone club queen counts full value, even though unguarded honors usually are not counted unless partner has bid the suit. By dou-bling one heart, North has in effect "bid" all the other suits.

If you hold 12 points but are uncertain of the best game spot, a cue-bid in the enemy suit will solve your problem. Example:

WEST	NORTH	EAST	SOUTH
1 ♣	double	pass	2 ♣

south could hold: (a) ♠ A 9 8 6   ♡ K 7 5 3   ◇ A 2   ♣ J 8 6
                       (b) ♠ A 10 2   ♡ A J 8   ◇ 10 8 5 4 3   ♣ A 2

(a) It would be injudicious to take a blind stab at game in a major suit, since you could pick the wrong one; and a jump response of two hearts or two spades would not be a safe way to buy time, since such a bid is not forcing. But the two-club cue-bid is the perfect answer.

(b) North could well hold a major suit that might provide the best game-going spot. By buying time with a cue-bid, you give North a chance to describe her hand, and if all else fails you can gamble it out in three notrump.

Rebids after a 12-point response　　If the doubler's partner bids game, the doubler passes unless interested in slam. Incidentally, it seldom pays to be ambitious in situations like the following:

EAST	SOUTH	WEST	NORTH
1 ◇	double	pass	4 ♠
pass	?		

south holds: ♠ A Q 9 7　♡ Q J 9 2　◇ A 10　♣ K Q 8

Although it contains strong spade support and a big point-count, this is not a slam-going hand. South undertook to deliver most of these features when she doubled one diamond; she merely has a few points to spare. On a somewhat stronger hand of the same type, the expert slam-going maneuver would be a cue-bid of five diamonds. In this situation, the cue-bid in the opponents' suit would be a slam try, indicating ace or void of diamonds.

When an opponent redoubles　　If your partner doubles for take-out and the next player redoubles, the chances are you will hold a very poor hand. The redouble will usually mean that the opponents hold more than half the deck and are fixing to double for penalties. It is therefore of paramount importance to locate a playable trump suit at the lowest possible level. And it may be desirable to show your suit over the redouble, even though in theory the redouble has relieved you from having to respond to the double. Example:

WEST	NORTH	EAST	SOUTH
1 ◇	double	redouble	?

south holds: (a) ♠ 8 6   ♡ J 6 4 3 2   ◇ J 5 3   ♣ 10 9 6
             (b) ♠ 10 8 7   ♡ 9 7 4   ◇ J 8   ♣ 10 8 7 3 2

(a) One heart. If South passed up the redouble, a rescue bid by North might go past the heart suit.

(b) South should pass the redouble. There will be plenty of time to bid clubs later if necessary. Meanwhile, North may get the team off the hook some other way.

Notrump responses to a double   It is important to realize that a one-notrump response is not a way to show a weak hand. (You can do that only by making a minimum bid in your cheapest suit.) One notrump is a *constructive* response, indicating 7-10 high-card points. Example:

WEST	NORTH	EAST	SOUTH
1 ♠	double	pass	1 NT

A typical hand for South would be:

♠ Q J 8 5   ♡ 9 2   ◇ K J 4   ♣ J 5 3 2

Regrettably, there are times when you have to break the rules and bid notrump on a weaker hand. Example:

WEST	NORTH	EAST	SOUTH
1 ♠	double	pass	?

south holds: ♠ K J 9 7   ♡ 5 2   ◇ 7 6 4 3   ♣ 8 5 2

South has a choice of rotten apples and one notrump is perhaps less bad than two diamonds, if only because it is the cheapest bid available. Although in theory the notrump bid shows 7-10 points, the doubler should try to allow leeway. Notice that this problem usually arises only when the opponents have opened a spade bid; over other bids, the doubler's partner will often be able to bid a suit at the one-level.

Jump responses in notrump are no problem. A response of two notrump usually indicates 11-12 points, while a leap to three shows 13 or more.

The penalty pass   There is just one type of hand on which you are permitted to pass a takeout double: when you figure you can score better by converting the takeout double into a penalty double. But—and this tendency is a slight feminine failing—don't take refuge in a penalty pass just because you have no attractive bid to make. The maneuver is seldom wise unless you hold at least five cards in the opponents' suit, and they should preferably be headed by a sequence such as K Q J or Q J 10. A penalty pass pays off best when you hold few high cards outside the trump suit, as in the following hand:

♠ Q J 10 8 4   ♡ 8 3   ◇ Q 10   ♣ 9 7 5 2

If your partner doubles an opening bid of one spade and the next hand passes, your best move is a penalty pass; the alternative call of two clubs could lead at best to a partial score and at worst to a substantial loss. But if you hold a stronger hand, you should think twice before passing; there may be a chance to make game your way. Example:

♠ A K Q 3   ♡ 10 2   ◇ J 9 7 5   ♣ 8 7 6

After one spade-double-pass, the best move would depend on

the vulnerability situation. Against vulnerable opponents, you could pass; but if you were vulnerable and the opponents were not, one notrump would be a better choice.

Balancing   Do women talk too much? That is the question we set out to research; and now that we are nearly through I still hold that, by and large, the opposite is true; women don't talk *enough* at the bridge table. But in the balancing position, it could be true: some women have a weakness for bargain-basement bids.

If your opponents' bidding fizzles at a low level, you have to decide whether to surrender or to go into competition for the contract. The basic situation arises when an opening is followed by two passes, as here:

WEST	NORTH	EAST	SOUTH
1 ◇	pass	pass	?

South is in a "balancing" position—which means she may elect to bid on a weaker hand than normal, on the presumption that North holds a reasonable quota of points. This presumption is a fair one, because East has shown a very weak hand by passing the opening bid. But although in a balancing position you are free to bid on scanty values, you shouldn't use this freedom too liberally. Like all freedoms, it works best when exercised with restraint. You must give your hand a long hard look before deciding to balance.

Some players don't pay much attention to balancing situations, figuring these are just partscore squabbles. This attitude is far from wise. The existence of a balancing scheme is a great comfort in competitive bidding, since it means you are not compelled to overcall every time you hold enough points to do so. It is perfectly possible to hold as many as 15 high-card points and yet have no safe overcall. If you pass, you are much happier if partner knows all about balancing and can be relied on to reopen the bidding on a suitable hand.

Balancing bids *are* bargain bids. For example, the count for a simple suit bid in the balancing position is only 8-13; with more, a takeout double or a jump bid is obligatory. Similarly, the points needed for a jump bid in a suit are cut to 12-16, and a balancing bid of one notrump shows only 11-14 instead of only 16-18.

The secret of successful balancing is to try to figure *why* your left-hand opponent's opening bid has been followed by two passes and *what* is likely to happen if you reopen. (The worst that can happen is that the opponents find a better fit in a new suit.)

WEST	NORTH	EAST	SOUTH
1♣	pass	pass	?

Should South bid on the following hand?

♠ 10 4 ♡ A Q 9 3 ◇ K 8 2 ♣ 10 9 6 2

South's strength is adequate for a bid of one heart—and, indeed, many players would make that bid. Nevertheless, a pass is a better call for two reasons: first, because South is short of spades, which enhances the danger that East-West may have a lock on that suit. Second, North has failed to take any action after West's easy-to-overcall one-club opening. North's silence could be because some of her strength is in clubs, a factor that argues in favor of leaving one club alone instead of giving East-West a chance to find a better spot. Should South balance on this hand?

WEST	NORTH	EAST	SOUTH
1♡	pass	pass	?

♠ J 8 6 5 2 ♡ A 8 5 ◇ K 10 ♣ 7 6 4

Undoubtedly South should bid one spade. It was much more difficult for North to overcall the one-heart opening than it was to overcall the one-club opening on the previous deal. Therefore North could hold quite a fair hand on which, for some reason or other, she could take no action. And since North-South hold the spade suit, it is unlikely that East-West will be able to outbid them.

Because a simple overcall can show a moderate hand in the balancing position, it is often advisable to jump the bidding on a hand that would be inadequate for such a maneuver in other circumstances. Example:

♠ 9 8 2   ♡ 5 3   ◊ A 10 7   ♣ A K Q 8 3

If your right-hand opponent opened one spade, you would bid just two clubs on this hand. But if the bidding is opened on your left and is followed by two passes, a jump to three clubs is quite in order.

A balancing bid of one notrump is strictly a low-gear bid, indicating 11-14 points in a hand that is unsuitable for a takeout double. You should double on all stronger hands, unless suitable for a jump bid or a forcing cue-bid in the opponents' suit. On three-suited hands with a shortage in the enemy suit, the double may be made on as little as 10 points.

My final tip is psychological rather than technical. Do not relax even when you have fully mastered the fine art of competitive bidding. There are still ways you can improve your game. When you have acquired a proficient technique, you should concentrate on producing every bid or pass with a smooth rhythm that gives nothing away to your opponents. That way, you will acquire the reputation of being a formidable opponent as well as a desirable partner.

Quizzes

QUIZ 1 You have to decide whether or not to overcall. Neither side vulnerable.

	south holds:		the bidding:		
			EAST	SOUTH	WEST	NORTH

1 ♠ A 7
♡ 3
◇ A J 7 5 4 2
♣ J 10 8 2

EAST	SOUTH	WEST	NORTH
1♡	?		

2 ♠ Q J 7
♡ 10 2
◇ Q 9 5
♣ A Q 8 6 3

NORTH	EAST	SOUTH	WEST
pass	1♠	?	

3 ♠ K 10
♡ Q 10 8 4 3 2
◇ K 2
♣ A 8 5

EAST	SOUTH	WEST	NORTH
1◇	?		

4 ♠ Q 7 5
♡ K J 8
◇ K J 9 3 2
♣ Q 5

NORTH	EAST	SOUTH	WEST
pass	1♣	?	

5 ♠ 8 5
♡ 6 5 3
◇ A K J 10 8
♣ 10 9 3

WEST	NORTH	EAST	SOUTH
1♠	pass	2♣	?

Answers

1 *Two diamonds.* Since the diamond suit lacks substance, there is some risk of being doubled. But this is more than outweighed by space factors—the two-diamond bid may stop West bidding spades.

2 *Pass.* A two-club overcall would be risky and has virtually no space value.

3 *One heart.* Admittedly the one-heart overcall will not shut West out, but South's general strength offers a good chance of buying the hand, especially as North has not yet passed. It is important to act quickly, otherwise the heart suit may be shut out by an enemy spade bid.

4 *Pass.* Since North failed to open the bidding, chances of buying the hand are not bright. A one-diamond overcall would be cheap but has little constructive purpose, and the most likely outcome would be to betray the location of your high cards to the eventual declarer.

5 *Two diamonds.* This gambit is a fair speculation with a perceptive partner, who will realize you may be bidding for lead-directing purposes rather than with any real hope of challenging for the final contract.

   QUIZ 2 Your partner has made a strong jump overcall, indicating around 17-19 points. What do you say? Both sides vulnerable.

south holds:		the bidding:		
		WEST	NORTH	EAST	SOUTH
1 ♠ Q J 10		1♡	2♠	pass	?
♡ K 5 2					
◇ 10 8 6 4					
♣ J 8 3					
		WEST	NORTH	EAST	SOUTH
2 ♠ A 2		1♡	3♣	pass	?
♡ Q 10 6					
◇ 10 7 5 4 3					
♣ Q 9 7					

south holds:

the bidding:

		WEST	NORTH	EAST	SOUTH
3	♠ A K 5 2				
	♡ J 10 7 5	1 ♡	3 ◇	pass	?
	◇ Q 8				
	♣ 6 3 2				

		WEST	NORTH	EAST	SOUTH
4	♠ 9 8 6 2				
	♡ A 2	1 ◇	2 ♠	3 ◇	?
	◇ 10 8 6				
	♣ Q J 10 3				

		WEST	NORTH	EAST	SOUTH
5	♠ K Q 10				
	♡ K J 8	1 ♣	2 ◇	pass	?
	◇ J 10 7 3				
	♣ 8 6 2				

Answers

1 *Pass.* It is unlikely your points are pulling their full weight. The heart king may prove little use, since West is expected to hold the ace; and although South holds good trump support, North probably does not expect to need any great help in that department.

2 *Three notrump.* North's jump overcall in a minor suit is likely to be based on maximum points, so with eight points in her own hand South should play for game. The club suit will probably run for six tricks, and any missing key cards are likely to be favorably located in West's hand.

3 *Three notrump.* It is unlikely a bid of three spades would pay off, since if North held four spades she would probably have doubled for takeout instead of bidding three diamonds. Better to launch straight into three notrump, concealing the spade suit, and taking a chance on not being wide open in clubs.

4 *Four spades.* When your right-hand opponent has made a com-

petitive raise, you should stop to consider whether a slight over-bid is in order. If you bid only *three* spades—which is all your hand would be worth had East passed—North may think you are bidding under pressure to contest the partial.

5 *Three clubs.* Holding 10 high-card points opposite a strong jump overcall, you are willing to contract for game, but an 11-trick contract in diamonds may not be best. By cue-bidding West's suit, South creates a game-forcing situation and gives North the chance to bid notrump if she holds a club guard.

QUIZ 3 Your partner has overcalled in a suit. What do you say? Neither side vulnerable.

south holds:

			the bidding:		
		WEST	NORTH	EAST	SOUTH
1	♠ K 10 ♡ 10 9 6 5 2 ◇ A K 5 2 ♣ 10 8	1♣	1♠	pass	?
2	♠ K J 6 ♡ Q 8 7 ◇ Q J 8 7 ♣ Q 9 2	1◇	1♡	pass	?
3	♠ J 9 ♡ A 8 5 3 ◇ A K 6 5 3 ♣ A 9	1♣	1♠	pass	?
4	♠ Q 10 9 2 ♡ K 10 8 7 ◇ 5 3 ♣ Q J 3	1♠	2♣	pass	?

	south holds:		**the bidding:**		
		WEST	**NORTH**	**EAST**	**SOUTH**
5	♠ 8 6	1 ◇	1 ♠	pass	?
	♡ K Q 10 8 4 3				
	◇ 8 6 5				
	♣ Q 8				

Answers

1 *Two spades.* Game is unlikely unless North holds a maximum overcall, but South can afford a single raise. You can safely support an overcall suit on K x, since partner is likely to hold at least a five-bagger.

2 *One notrump.* This time South holds stronger support for North's suit than she did in the previous problem, but a notrump takeout is preferred to a raise of North's suit, since it better describes the character of the hand. Notice that a notrump response to an overcall shows appreciably more points than it would show in response to an *opening* bid.

3 *Three diamonds.* South does not hold primary support for North's suit, but her points are all in "quickies." Game should be a fair gamble but it could be unwise to leap straight to four spades or three notrump, either of which could be the wrong spot. By forcing with three diamonds, South gives North a second chance to describe her hand; North might even bid hearts.

4 *Pass.* With strong holdings in both major suits, it is unlikely East-West can make game. The danger in raising to three clubs is that it might stimulate North to contest the bidding too vigorously.

5 *Two hearts.* After partner has overcalled, a simple change of suit is not forcing; it is therefore the marked bid, even though South holds only seven high-card points.

QUIZ 4 You have to decide whether to double for takeout. What do you say? Neither side vulnerable.

south holds:		the bidding:			
1 ♠ K 10 8 7 3		EAST	SOUTH	WEST	NORTH
♡ K 6		1 ♣	?		
◇ A K 8 7					
♣ 6 5					
2 ♠ Q J 8 5		NORTH	EAST	SOUTH	WEST
♡ A Q J 10		pass	1 ◇	?	
◇ 8 6					
♣ J 8 7					
3 ♠ 8		EAST	SOUTH	WEST	NORTH
♡ 8 7 3 2		1 ♠	?		
◇ A K J 9 5					
♣ A 6 3					
4 ♠ A Q		WEST	NORTH	EAST	SOUTH
♡ K 6 3 2		pass	pass	1 ♠	?
◇ A Q 9 5					
♣ Q 9 4					
5 ♠ K 7		NORTH	EAST	SOUTH	WEST
♡ K J 9		pass	1 ♡	?	
◇ A J 10 3					
♣ A Q J 4					

Answers

1 *One spade*. While I would not condemn a takeout double, the one-spade overcall is slightly superior in that it may well shut out an enemy heart contract.

2 *Double.* Again South has to make a knife-edge decision. I find no fault with any South who prefers to remain silent, and I can see some virtue in a one-heart overcall, which has considerable lead-directing value. Nevertheless, my personal preference is for the double, since the hand contains two strong four-card majors and therefore has offensive potential even though North failed to open the bidding.

3 *Double.* At first sight it seems attractive to bid diamonds, but the temptation should be resisted. Our four small hearts could be a more important feature than the strong diamond suit; if North happens to hold four hearts this will be the best spot to play in. And only a takeout double is likely to persuade North to bid a weak heart suit.

4 *One notrump.* A double would not be bad, but the notrump overcall has the edge, since it tells North we hold 16-18 points. And North can still probe for a heart game by bidding a Stayman two clubs, just as after a notrump opening.

5 *Double.* Even though South lacks support for the unbid major suit, the double is the only accurate call since the hand is too strong for a one-notrump overcall. If North responds one spade, a notrump rebid by South will reveal precisely this type of hand.

QUIZ 5 Your partner has doubled for takeout. What do you say? Neither side vulnerable.

south holds:		the bidding:		
		WEST	NORTH	EAST	SOUTH

1 ♠ Q 8 3 2

   ♡ 9 4 3

   ◇ K 6

   ♣ A J 10 7

	WEST	NORTH	EAST	SOUTH
	1♡	double	pass	?

2 ♠ J 10 6 2

   ♡ A 8 4 3

   ◇ A 5

   ♣ K 8 6

	WEST	NORTH	EAST	SOUTH
	1◇	double	2◇	?

	south holds:		the bidding:			
			WEST	**NORTH**	**EAST**	**SOUTH**
3	♠ Q J 6					
	♡ 4 2		1 ◇	double	pass	?
	◇ 9 7 5 3 2					
	♣ 8 6 5					
			WEST	**NORTH**	**EAST**	**SOUTH**
4	♠ Q J 8 5					
	♡ K 5		1 ♠	double	pass	?
	◇ 10 6 4 2					
	♣ K J 7					
			WEST	**NORTH**	**EAST**	**SOUTH**
5	♠ J 8 7 5					
	♡ 9 7 2		1 ♡	double	4 ♡	?
	◇ K Q 10 4					
	♣ Q 2					

Answers

1 *Two spades*. With 9-11 points plus four cards in the vital spade suit, a jump response is in order. Notice that although South's clubs are stronger than her spades, the major-suit response is best.

2 *Three diamonds*. 12 high-card points plus the certainty of a fit in one of the major suits entitle South to issue a game-going signal. Instead of taking a blind guess which major suit to bid, South ensures finding the best spot by cue-bidding the opponents' suit.

3 *One spade*. Although South has a headache, she must not pass the double, since she does not have a strong enough diamond holding. North has asked for South's best suit and she must do her duty, even though this entails bidding a three-card suit. A one-notrump response to the double would show a stronger hand.

4 *One notrump*. This time South is thankful that the notrump response is a special bid, indicating 7-10 high-card points. Without

such an arrangement, South would have no good bid available. 5 *Four spades*. Opponents tend to preempt to the limit after a takeout double, and it generally pays to accept the challenge by going for game instead of for a penalty. In view of the vigorous E-W bidding, it is likely North holds a minimum number of points for her takeout double; this in turn makes it likely she holds a three-suited hand to compensate for a shortage of points, so South can be sure she'll find four-card spade support in North's hand.

QUIZ 6 You have doubled for takeout. What do you say on the next round? Both sides vulnerable.

south holds:	the bidding:			
1 ♠ 9 7	EAST	SOUTH	WEST	NORTH
♡ K Q J 3	1 ♠	double	pass	2 ♣
◊ A 7 3 2	pass	?		
♣ Q 10 5				
2 ♠ A K J 8 3	EAST	SOUTH	WEST	NORTH
♡ A 10 8	1 ♡	double	pass	2 ♣
◊ A K 10	pass	?		
♣ 5 2				
3 ♠ K Q 8 2	EAST	SOUTH	WEST	NORTH
♡ A K J	1 ♣	double	pass	1NT
◊ K J 5 4 2	pass	?		
♣ 5				
4 ♠ A Q 2	EAST	SOUTH	WEST	NORTH
♡ A Q 10 8	1 ♠	double	pass	3 ♣
◊ 10 5 4	pass	?		
♣ Q 10 8				

south holds:		the bidding:			
5	♠ A 10 8 6	EAST	SOUTH	WEST	NORTH
	♡ 6 3 2	1♡	double	2♡	2♠
	◇ A 8	3♡	?		
	♣ A K 10 3				

Answers

1 *Pass.* South has already shown her hand by doubling for takeout. Any further bid by South would promise non-existent strength.

2 *Two spades.* Even on this very powerful hand, there is no need to bid more than two spades. We have to remember that North's two-club bid was forced and could be based on a Yarborough.

3 *Two notrump.* North probably holds 7-10 points, so there is a chance to make game if she is near a maximum. South should resist the temptation to bid diamonds, preferring to raise notrump even though she holds a small singleton in East's club suit. South has already indicated a club shortage by doubling one club for takeout, and if North chooses to bid notrump it is North's party.

4 *Three notrump.* South holds a close-to-minimum double, but three notrump can sometimes be wrapped up with less than the usual number of high-card points. South's tenaces in the major suits can be upgraded, since the major-suit kings are expected to be well placed in East's hand. It would not be wise to bid three hearts, since this would tend to pinpoint South's diamond weakness and attract a damaging lead in that suit.

5 *Four spades.* Somewhat of an overbid, but South has two things going for her. Now that hearts have been supported, it is likely North holds a singleton; furthermore, if South bids only *three* spades, North may think she is under pressure and may pass.

QUIZ 7   Although you have bid a suit in response to North's takeout double, she has failed to support it. What do you say now? North-South vulnerable.

south holds:		**the bidding:**		
		WEST	NORTH	EAST	SOUTH

1 ♠ 10 9 7 3
   ♡ J 5
   ♢ Q 10 5 2
   ♣ A 10 8

	WEST	NORTH	EAST	SOUTH
	1♡	double	pass	1♠
	pass	1NT	pass	?

2 ♠ A Q 10 8
   ♡ 5 3 2
   ♢ Q 10 2
   ♣ Q 9 8

	WEST	NORTH	EAST	SOUTH
	1♢	double	pass	2♠
	pass	3♣	pass	?

3 ♠ Q J
   ♡ 8 7 5
   ♢ K 10 9
   ♣ 10 7 5 4 3

	WEST	NORTH	EAST	SOUTH
	1♡	double	pass	2♣
	pass	2♠	pass	?

south holds: **the bidding:**

4 ♠ A 10 7 5 3
   ♡ 7 6 3 2
   ♢ A 2
   ♣ 9 5

	WEST	NORTH	EAST	SOUTH
	1♣	double	pass	2♠
	pass	3♣	pass	?

5 ♠ 8 5 2
   ♡ 6
   ♢ 10 7 2
   ♣ Q J 8 7 4 2

	WEST	NORTH	EAST	SOUTH
	1♢	double	pass	2♣
	pass	2♡	pass	?

Answers

1 *Three notrump*. Since North lacks support for the unbid major suit, she must hold a strong double, particularly since the vulnerability situation is unfavorable. The only explanation that fits is that North holds 19 points up—too many for an immediate one-notrump overcall.

2 *Three notrump*. South was quite right to jump to two spades

on only 10 points, since this bid, although encouraging, is not forcing. But North's rebid in a new suit creates a forcing situation and she must not be left stranded. Therefore we should bid notrump even though our guard in West's suit is not strong.

3 *Three spades.* The likely explanation of North's maneuver is that she holds a substantial point-count, plus a five-card spade suit that was not suitable for a two-spade overcall. South's spade honors are precious, and since she might have made the same two-club response on a bust hand, South has full values for a spade raise.

4 *Three hearts.* The meaning of North's cue-bid in West's suit is that she wants to play for game but is unsure of the best spot. The three-heart bid on a very weak suit is likely to be much more helpful than an unimaginative spade rebid, since North may also hold a weak four-card heart suit.

5 *Three clubs.* North is probably hoping we can show preference for one of the major suits, but we are unable to oblige. It is hardly possible that there is a better spot to play in than clubs.

QUIZ 8   You are in a balancing position. What do you say? Neither side vulnerable.

south holds:		the bidding:		
		WEST	NORTH	EAST	SOUTH
1	♠ Q 8 3	1♠	pass	pass	?
	♡ J 7 2				
	◇ K J 7				
	♣ A Q 9 5				
2	♠ A 9 8	WEST	NORTH	EAST	SOUTH
	♡ A 2	1♣	pass	pass	?
	◇ J 8 7 3				
	♣ J 10 6 4				
3	♠ A Q 3 2	WEST	NORTH	EAST	SOUTH
	♡ 8 6	1♡	pass	pass	?
	◇ Q 7 5 2				
	♣ K 9 6				

south holds:		the bidding:		
		WEST	NORTH	EAST	SOUTH

4 ♠ 5 4
  ♡ 8 3 2
  ◇ A Q 9
  ♣ A K Q 3 2

	WEST	NORTH	EAST	SOUTH
	1 ♠	pass	pass	?

5 ♠ Q 8 6 4 2
  ♡ 10 6
  ◇ A J 9
  ♣ 6 5 3

	WEST	NORTH	EAST	SOUTH
	1 ♣	pass	pass	?

Answers

1 *One notrump.* Holding the correct count for a balancing bid in notrump—11-14 points—South should not be put off by the fact that her spade guard is somewhat sketchy; indeed, it can be profitable to bid notrump in the balancing position even if you hold no stop in the enemy suit. This is a less dangerous maneuver than doubling with the wrong distribution or bidding two clubs on a four-card suit.

2 *Pass.* One club is not a difficult opening to overcall. North's pass may therefore be due either to the fact that she holds few points or that she holds club strength. In both cases South is likely to do best by leaving West undisturbed.

3 *Double.* South's hand would be at least two points shy of a takeout double in a normal situation, but in the balancing position it is adequate. The double is preferable to a bid of one spade, since the latter could be made on as few as 8 points.

4 *Three clubs.* 13 points is the normal maximum for a simple overcall in the balancing position. With 15 points in high cards alone, South should make a show of strength, hoping this will nudge North in the direction of three notrump.

5 *One spade.* A minimum hand for the bid. If the long suit were not spades, South would be better advised to pass.

Mary Jane Farell

Women's first-ranking master point player

Long before the summer of 1964, when she took over the top spot as the world's leading master point winner among women—she stands fifth in the all-time ranking of men and women—Mary Jane Farell had earned a title she values more than any of the others: the most ethical, the most courteous and the nicest opponent one could meet. And the best partner.

Mary Jane is an eminent teacher, whose record of success disproves once and for all the snide witticism: "Those who can't, teach." Her most recent notable victory was in the World Mixed Pair Olympiad 1966, at Amsterdam (with Ivan Erdos). She also finished third in the Women's Pair event in that same Olympiad, playing as partner of Peggy Solomon, and thereby became the biggest contributor toward the United States entry's winning the Charles J. Solomon trophy for best performance of any nation in the tourney.

Brilliant when the time comes for brilliance, but always a sound and steady player, Mary Jane's preemptive bids make life easy for partner but difficult for opponents. Mary Jane shares with you, in her fine chapter on preemptive bidding, some inside tips on how to overcome the feminine tendency toward over-economical bids.

The Precarious Preempt

**By controlling bargain-hunting
instincts, women can make bids
that pay off ... by Mary Jane Farell**

The surest way to stir up some action in a bridge game is with a preempt—opening with a shutout bid of three in a suit. This simple maneuver can create problems that are far from simple for your opponents to solve.

Here's why: Your partner (as do your opponents) knows what you have and it is easy for him to estimate the value of your combined hands. But your opponents are trying to figure out how the rest of the cards are divided among three hands—and they have to do their guessing with uncomfortably little space left for exploration.

Because shutouts are designed to brave a possible penalty double, a false impression has gotten around that all you need to open a three-bid is a long suit and stout nerves. In truth, however, some very subtle qualities come into play—chiefly table presence. And, since women are strong on knowing what's going on around them, we can shine in shutout bidding, provided we can conquer a feminine yen for ultra-economical bids.

Don't Look for Bargains

Most bidders tend to assume that the best call in any given situation is the call that can be made at the cheapest possible level. And since women are keen bargain-hunters, they are usually very willing to espouse this bargain approach to bidding.

Unfortunately, space-saving bids aren't always as economical as might seem; when a player saves space for herself she automatically saves it for her opponents too. On some deals the opponents can make more profitable use of this space than you can; then bargain bids may simply help the opponents to bid more accurately.

Good shutout bidding—which can be defined as the art of wasting space profitably—aims to prevent this.

The 500 Rule

You can start making three-bids as soon as you start playing bridge—provided you stick pretty closely to the 500 Rule. This is founded on the proposition that it is a fair trade to go down 500 points to save an enemy game contract, so a non-vulnerable player can open three on any hand which contains six probable tricks and less than the 13 points that are normally needed for an opening bid. If you hold 13 points, your proper opening is a normal bid of one. Example:

(a) ♠ Q J 8 7 5 4 3   ♡ 7   ◇ K Q 2   ♣ 8 6
(b) ♠ A J 10 7 6 2   ♡ A Q 7   ◇ 8 3   ♣ 9 7

Hand (a) is a mint specimen for a non-vulnerable three opening; on a normal distribution of the outstanding cards you should win five spade tricks and one diamond. Thus, if you are doubled for penalty you should not be set more than three tricks, not vulnerable, thus conforming precisely to the 500 Rule.

Hand (b), however, is not a valid three opening, for as well as six probable playing tricks it also contains 13 points in high cards and distribution. It should therefore be opened with a bid of one since, as we shall see later, partner will assume on a three-bid that you do not hold enough points to open one.

(c) ♠ K Q J 10 8 3 2   ♡ 8   ◇ 7   ♣ Q J 10 3

With six spade tricks and an establishable trick in clubs, this hand is worth a *vulnerable* three-bid. If doubled, you should go down two, or just 500 points—a fair trade against the game or slam that your opponents could presumably have made.

Notice that if a hand is good enough for a vulnerable three opening this automatically means it is not suitable for a non-vulnerable bid at the same level. Thus you would not open three spades on hand (c) if you were not vulnerable, since partner would expect one trick less and might well pass up a hand that held sufficient strength to make game. Not vulnerable, therefore, you would open *four* spades.

The fact that three-bids have a top and bottom limit means that in some ways they are a more accurate tool than other open-ings. On an opening bid of one of a suit you know only that the opener holds 13 points up, plus a biddable suit. Since the top limit is very high, the actual trick-taking potential of the combined hands may be hard to find out. But on an opening three-bid, you know opener does not hold more than 12 points, and also that she holds about six or seven probable tricks, according to vulner-ability. This makes it possible to respond very accurately.

Because a preemptive bid aims to shut out the opponents, it would normally be tops in wasted effort to open such a bid in fourth position after both opponents had already passed. By the same reasoning, it is quite possible to hold a borderline hand that would be worth a three-bid in first or third position but not in second position. In second position a three-bid is less purposeful, since one opponent has already passed but your partner has not; the odds now say that the deal belongs to you rather than to your opponents.

You can buck the 500 Rule

Although in many of life's more precarious activities the higher you fly the harder you fall, this does not apply to shutout bidding. Every good preemptive opening has its own safety harness that makes sure you are unlikely to fall farther than a predetermined distance. And although, according to the classic teaching of bridge theorists, that distance is exactly 500 points, experienced players find it highly profitable occasionally to stretch the figure. In other words, they open three on many hands that do not contain the regulation number of tricks—but they have a reason for so doing.

The 500 Rule is somewhat pessimistic in that it assumes you *will* go down 500 every time you stop your opponents making game. It overlooks the fact that by timing your shutout bids well, you can frequently save a game *without it costing you anything.* When this happens, you make a very handsome profit indeed, which means you can actually afford to go down more than 500 on some other deals. Therefore, provided you possess keen judgment, you can open a three-bid on many hands that do not contain quite as many playing tricks as the 500 Rule demands.

The 500 Rule would pan out accurately if opponents always took winning action—for example, if they always doubled a three-bid when they held strong hands on which they couldn't score game, and always bid to their own best spot when they could not extract an adequate penalty by doubling.

It is, however, quite impossible for any team to take consistently correct action in these situations, as the following deal from a team championship shows.

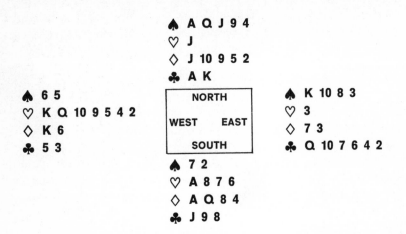

In Room 1 the bidding, with both sides vulnerable, went:

WEST	NORTH	EAST	SOUTH
3♡	3♠	pass	3NT
pass	pass	pass	

West opened the king of hearts, continuing the suit when South ducked. There being no advantage in holding up any more, South won the ace on the second round and took the spade finesse, losing to East's king. East put the declarer on the spot by returning a diamond and South, who realized nine tricks were unlikely to roll in unless the diamond finesse was right, played low. West now won the diamond king and cashed out the heart suit, setting the contract 400 points.

South could have salvaged two or three tricks had she elected to go in with the diamond ace instead of risking the finesse, but she could not have made her contract. And although hindsight suggests that four spades might have been a better bid for South to make than three notrump, it could easily have been the wrong move on a different layout. Furthermore, the best game spot for North-South—five diamonds—was practically unattainable via normal bidding, because West's three-heart opening had consumed too much space.

When the deal was replayed in Room 2, West timidly declined to open a vulnerable three-bid because he held only about six playing tricks—one fewer than the 500 Rule requires. After West had passed, North opened one spade and South bid a routine two diamonds. West now ventured a butt-in of two hearts, but the boat had already sailed. North-South easily brushed aside all interference and reached an unbeatable five-diamond contract to rack up a 600 score.

The total swing was 1000 points to the team that opened three hearts—and even the most hard-bitten accountant would agree that some of the profits from this kind of bonanza are available to help pay the losses on the relatively few occasions when a preemptive bid is doubled for more than a 500 penalty. It is true that one can sometimes be hit in a three-bid when the opponents, because of a perverse layout of the cards, could not have made a game. But most experts hold that the advantage is still heavily in favor of prolific three-bids.

This is why experts often jettison the 500 Rule, especially when not vulnerable. A hand from the World Team Championship provides a dramatic example.

♠ Q J 9 8 6 4   ♡ —   ◇ 10 9 7 4 3 2   ♣ 10

If you disregard the chance of building some tricks in diamonds, this hand contains only three—or at most four—probable tricks. Yet the British and North American players both opened three spades, and bustled their opponents into an unmakeable four hearts instead of a laydown three notrump. Notice that a key factor in favor of the "risky" three-spade bid is the presence of a second suit, which tends to boost the chances of a lucky result.

It is unusual, of course, to possess a concealed five- or six-card suit when you open a three-bid, but it is not uncommon to hold a four-card minor suit. And such a holding makes it much more difficult for your opponents to pin a really damaging penalty on you. Consider the following very common situation:

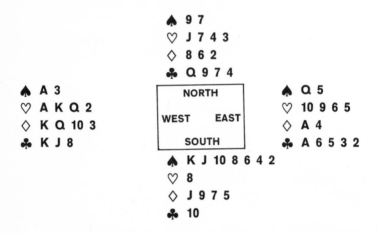

South is in three spades doubled, having opened with a non-vulnerable preemptive bid. West leads hearts and, after ruffing the second round, South has to consider what to play next.

If she tackled trumps from her own hand, South would lose to both the ace and the queen, winning only five tricks in all and suffering a 700 set. But although there seems to be no chance to compensate by developing a long card in the four-card diamond suit, that suit can still play a part.

Having ruffed the second heart lead, South plays diamonds. Sooner or later, the defenders will either have to let South ruff the fourth diamond on the table—thus ensuring a sixth trick that will hold the penalty to a reasonable 500 number—or they will have to lead trumps to kill dummy's ruffing potential. This will give South the chance to take the winning finesse against East's queen, again holding the penalty to 500. Thus, the "useless" diamond suit is in fact worth a trick.

But although a four-card *minor* suit is a good backstop to a three-bid, it is dangerous to keep a four-card major suit up your sleeve. One can easily miss game by opening three spades on:

♠ A J 9 7 4 3 2 ♡ K 8 5 2 ◇ 9 6 ♣ —

If partner holds an average hand that includes a four-card heart suit, the heart game probably will be your best spot. But you won't get there if you open three spades,* since there is no way to fish for a four-four fit after a three-opening. Therefore you either pass or open one spade, depending on whether you favor a bold or cautious style.

The rank of the main suit is another key factor in the decision whether to open three on a borderline hand. Since the minor suits are zero stopping power, good bidders may pass up a minor-suit hand that superficially is worth a three-bid. Example:

♠ A J 7 ♡ 10 2 ◇ 9 ♣ Q 10 8 7 6 4 3

If you open three clubs, you have less chance to shut out an adverse game contract than you would have if your suit were spades—but you have exactly the same chance to incur a costly penalty. Since the hand is merely borderline, it is better to pass because the long suit is the *wrong* suit.

My next tip concerns three-openings in fourth position. Although these are uncommon, they are not unknown, especially when the opposition have the reputation of being highly competitive bidders. Suppose you hold the following hand in fourth position.

♠ 8 3 ♡ 6 5 ◇ K J 7 ♣ A K J 10 5 3

---

* *Four spades if not vulnerable.*

Against keen opponents, it is quite a good idea to open three clubs, since if you open a normal one-club bid they are almost certain to contest in a major suit. Chances are you will be forced to the three-level anyway—and if the opponents strike a lucky enough fit you may even be outbid. By opening three clubs, you increase your chances of buying the hand, and partner will usually leave you undisturbed unless she holds a maximum pass plus a fit in your suit.

Responding to Three-Bids

Three-bids are aimed primarily at shutting out the opponents, but they also pin a large "Do Not Disturb" notice on the responder, who is not expected to take action unless she can supply more than the number of tricks by which opener has deliberately over-bid her hand. Example: if partner opens a non-vulnerable three-heart bid, you do not expect her to deliver more than six tricks, so you need to hold *more* than three tricks yourself before you can raise.

Furthermore, to be worth anything your tricks have to be aces and kings that will provide fast winners no matter what hand pattern your partner may hold. When distributional storms are howling, queens and jacks are unlikely to be of interest. All in all, you can usually forget about disturbing a non-vulnerable three-opening unless you hold about 15 high-card points, mainly in aces and kings. But opposite a vulnerable three-bid, 12 points may be enough.

After a three-bid, it seldom pays to shop around for a different suit to play in, since partner's hand may be useless unless played in her suit. So the problem of valuing the responding hand is largely the problem of assessing its suitability for a raise of opener's suit—a task that can be somewhat of a guessing game unless you know the right technique.

I have a special way of raising three-bids that works very

accurately. On a non-vulnerable three-opening, I place my partner
with a seven-card suit that has two gaps in it. And on a vulnerable opening, I place her with a seven-card suit that has only one
gap. This allows for the possibility that partner's three-opening
does not quite measure up to the 500 Rule. I now play the hand
through mentally, placing my actual hand opposite partner's
imaginary hand, and try to figure whether a game is likely to be a
fifty-fifty chance or better.

Using this technique, the responses fall readily into place.
Suppose, with neither side vulnerable, your partner opens three
spades and you hold the following:

♠ J 5   ♡ K Q 10 4   ◇ Q 10 7 4   ♣ A 8 6

You start by placing partner with a seven-card spade suit
that has two gaps in it; and since you happen to hold the jack it
is possible your partner holds, say, ♠ K Q 10 x x x x. (If you
happened to hold the king yourself, you would probably place
partner with ♠ Q J 10 x x x x.)

Next, you assume partner holds two small cards in each of
the plain suits, which means her hand is something like this:

♠ K Q 10 x x x x   ♡ x x   ◇ x x   ♣ x x

Clearly there is a danger that partner will lose two diamonds,
a club and a heart, as well as the trump ace in which case she
will be set one trick in her contract of three spades. If the defenders fail to lead clubs early enough, or if partner holds an extra
high card such as the club or diamond king, she may land the
partial, but obviously you do not hold enough in aces and kings
to justify a raise to four spades. Another example:

♠ A K 6 2   ♡ 3   ◇ 10 9 7   ♣ A K 7 6 4

This time you are vulnerable. Therefore, when partner opens three hearts you are worth a raise to four even though you have only a small single trump, because you do not expect more than one gap in the trump suit. Partner's hand should be something like this:

♠ x x   ♡ K Q J 10 x x x   ◇ x x   ♣ x x

She may of course hold an extra high card somewhere, but even though we cautiously disregard that possibility, a raise to game should be pretty safe. But notice that a three-notrump contract would be a mess, even if we were not wide open in diamonds, since we would never be able to bring in the heart suit.

However, this same technique *can* be used to consider—or reject—a bid of notrump. Suppose partner opens a vulnerable three-club bid and you hold the following:

♠ A 2   ♡ K 10 8 4   ◇ K Q J 9   ♣ 8 6 3

Since partner might hold as many as seven playing tricks, you are naturally tempted to convert to three notrump, but this is a dangerous gamble. There is expected to be a hole in the club suit, and your contract would be wrecked by a spade opening lead. The "automatic" three-notrump bid should therefore be rejected; it is wiser to settle for the safe club partial, in which partner will probably net nine or ten tricks.

Although you usually need 12-15 points in high cards to raise a preempt, there are some special situations where you can raise on very few points—or, indeed, on no points at all. A raise of this type is called an advance sacrifice, and is made when you are weak on defense. Example:

♠ Q 7 4   ♡ 6   ◇ K 10 5 3 2   ♣ 10 8 6 3

When partner opens three spades, it is a safe bet your opponents can make game, if not slam. So if your right-hand opponent happens to pass, you should not do the same, hoping for the miracle that the fourth-hand player will pass too. Instead, you should raise to four spades. This is much better than waiting for your opponents to bid game, since by that time they may have assembled enough information to bid a slam.

Last on the list of problems that partner's three-opening can pin on you is what to do over an opponent's overcall. This needs careful handling, because it is from this type of situation that many of your profits are expected to come. Example:

NORTH	EAST	SOUTH	WEST
3 ◇	3 ♡	?	

south holds: ♠ A 6 ♡ Q J 8 5 ◇ 8 3 2 ♣ A Q 10 7

The three-heart overcall is very favorable to North-South; East probably will not win more than eight tricks in a heart contract. The expected profit, however, stems not so much from the possibility that East may concede a small minus, but from the chance that East-West may miss game in spades. (North would not open three diamonds if she held a four-card spade suit, so East-West must hold at least eight spades between them.)

In a situation like this, your prime concern is to do nothing to help your opponents locate a better spot. Therefore you should not double an overcall that is short of game unless you are prepared to double any other suit that your opponents may retreat to. The invisible profit you expect to win via the missed spade game is much more important than the extra figures you might score via a penalty double of three hearts, even if you could make such a double stick. Indeed, you might even consider a raise to four diamonds!

If you pass up the chance to double overcalls like the above, you'll be surprised how often you'll get the chance to double the same suit at a higher level. Part of the dilemma that confronts a player whose partner overcalls a preemptive opening is that he has very little idea how strong the overcall suit is. Sometimes he will raise on what proves to be inadequate trump support.

Four-Bids

Sometimes you will pick up a hand that is weak on defense but contains too many tricks for a three-bid. In such a case, the solution may be an opening bid of four. Not vulnerable, both the following hands would be worth a four-bid.

(a) ♠ 8 6   ♡ 3   ◇ K Q J 10 7 6 4 3   ♣ J 8
(b) ♠ 9   ♡ K Q J 9 8 4 3   ◇ Q J 9   ♣ 6 2

Each hand contains about seven tricks—one more than is needed for a non-vulnerable bid of three. Of course, if you were *vulnerable,* you would open with a normal bid of three, since then the trick-taking potential would tie in exactly with the 500 Rule.

We saw earlier that you can sometimes open a three-bid on a hand that is short on the regulation number of tricks. With four-bids, it is just the opposite, since here you can sometimes open with a game bid in a major suit on a hand that is superficially *too strong* in high-card points. Example:

♠ A K Q J 5 3 2   ♡ 7   ◇ K Q 10   ♣ 6 4

You are vulnerable and your opponents are not. It is highly unlikely that there is any better spot than spades, so it is quite a good idea to open with a game bid in that suit, even though you have more than enough strength for a bid of one spade. The object, of course, is to prevent your non-vulnerable opponents from getting together and locating a cheap save.

Responding to four-bids is easier than responding to three-bids. If the opening bid is in a minor suit, you can assume partner has overbid by exactly two or three tricks, depending on the vulnerability, and you can act accordingly. And if the opening bid is in a major suit, you do not need to disturb it at all—unless, of course, you want to make a slam try. In this case, any new-suit bid shows the ace of that suit. Example:

♠ J 3   ♡ A Q 4   ♢ J 10 9   ♣ A K 7 6 4

When partner opens four spades you can envision a possible slam if she can look after the diamond suit. If you are not the sort of player who is prepared to bid a brash six spades direct, you can make a probing bid of five clubs. Partner will understand this is a slam try, showing control of clubs, and on a suitable hand she may cooperate by bidding five diamonds. This probing procedure is better than taking off into a Blackwood sequence, because it may enable you to bid slam when partner holds a diamond void or singleton.

Defending Against the Three-Bid

Big-league bridgers are no shy violets, anxious to sidestep the spotlight. But for many such experts, the last little prayer at night is that they will have a poor hand the next time an opponent opens a three-bid. Only then will they have no problems. The sad truth is that there is no sure-fire defense against the three-bid opener.

Most experts hold that the best way to cope with an enemy three-bid is to take the same action that you would take against a bid of one. They use the double of a three-bid for takeout—though on a suitable hand partner can pass for penalties. Naturally, you need to be better upholstered in terms of points before taking action against a three-bid than against a one-bid. Therefore I have developed what I call the 1-2-3 Rule, which works well against all types of preemptive openings.

The 1-2-3 Rule means simply that you need that many more points to take action against a shutout bid than you would need if the opening bid were at the level of one. Therefore, since the minimum strength needed for a takeout double or a genuine over-call at the one level is 13 points, you need 14–one point extra–to take the same action against a *two*-bid. Similarly, you need 15–*two* points extra–against a *three*-bid. And you need 16–*three* points extra–against a *four*-bid.

Since we are at present considering only the defense against three-bids, here is an example to show how the 1-2-3 Rule works against such an opening. Your opponent opens three hearts and you hold:

♠ Q 8 5 3   ♡ 7   ◇ A 10 9 2   ♣ A Q J 4

You have the right pattern for a takeout double—but do you hold enough points? Yes, you do. With two points less, you would still have just enough for a double of *one* heart, so on the actual hand you can with your 15 points double three hearts. With four-card support for each of the unbid suits, the distributional pattern is ideal, but if the hand pattern were less than classic, you would need extra points to compensate.

Beware of hands where you want to double for penalties. It is usually better to pass unless you are strong enough to bid no-trump. Suppose there is a three-spade opening on your right and you hold:

(a)   ♠ K Q 9 2   ♡ 7 3   ◇ A K 6   ♣ Q 10 5 3
(b)   ♠ K Q 5 3   ♡ J 5   ◇ K Q J 9   ♣ A Q 8

Hand (a) would be worth a penalty double of three spades—if you could make it stick. Unfortunately, partner would interpret a double as a takeout request and would probably make an unwelcome response in hearts. The only sane action, therefore, is to pass, hoping partner can dredge up a takeout double which we can leave in. Notice that the point count is insufficient for a bid of three notrump, since the Rule of 1-2-3 indicates that you need 18 points—two more than are needed for a one-notrump overcall.

Hand (b) is again unsuitable for a double of three spades but, with 19 points, it is strong enough for a bid of three notrump. Naturally you probably won't make three notrump unless partner holds a fair share of the missing points, but you are entitled to bid on the assumption that she does hold that share.

I recommend the same 1-2-3 Rule when considering a suit overcall of an enemy three opening. Since the usual minimum for a genuine overcall of a one-bid is 13 points, you therefore need 15 for an overcall of a three-bid—and of course you also need a strong five-card suit. The following hand would be about right for a bid of three spades over an enemy three opening:

♠ A Q J 5 3   ♡ A 2   ◇ J 8 6   ♣ K 7 4

You may be wondering why, in gauging whether to take action against an enemy three-opening, I apparently ignore the vulnerability situation. "Surely," you may argue, "more points are needed for a vulnerable overcall, especially when the opponents are not vulnerable."

There is indeed a school of thought which holds that view but there is also a school which does not. Aggressive opponents take careful notice of the vulnerability situation, and when your team only is vulnerable they will open three-bids on little more than hope. If, in this situation, you refuse to enter the fray without extra points for vulnerability, the opponents will get away with murder far too often.

There is a different consideration which should cause you to vary the strength of your doubles and overcalls—the positional factor. If an enemy three-bid on your left is followed by two passes, you can enter the auction on a weaker hand, because you know that the partner of the three-bidder does not hold too much strength. This factor enables us to abandon the 1-2-3 Rule and bid on the same strength hand as against an enemy one-bid. Suppose you are South in the following situation:

WEST	NORTH	EAST	SOUTH
3 ◇	pass	pass	?

you hold: (a) ♠ Q 10 7 3   ♡ K 9 7 5   ◇ 8 6   ♣ A K J
          (b) ♠ 9 4   ♡ A J 10 7 3   ◇ A 10 2   ♣ K 6 4
          (c) ♠ J 6 4   ♡ K 2   ◇ A Q 5   ♣ A Q J 8 3

Hand (a) is just strong enough for a normal double of one diamond. It is therefore worth a double of three diamonds in fourth position.

Hand (b) would indicate a heart overcall at the one level. Because of the bidding it therefore rates a three-heart bid.

Hand (c) is a standard one-notrump opening or overcall. It therefore earns the three-notrump vote after a three-opening and two passes.

Action against other preemptive openings   In addition to weak three-openings, you will encounter barrage bids of four and, from some opponents, weak two-bids as well. Against weak two-openings I recommend the same defensive operation as against three-bids, with the difference that the extra strength needed for a double or an overcall can be shaved to one point in accordance with the 1-2-3 Rule. And of course against an opening bid of *four*, you need three points more than you would need against an opening bid of one. But over a four-bid, a double is less of a takeout request and more of a cooperative penalty double. This means partner should leave the double in on balanced hands, taking out only when he holds a long suit that is likely to yield game. Example:

WEST	NORTH	EAST	SOUTH
4♡	double	pass	?

(a)   ♠ Q 5 3   ♡ 9 8 2   ◇ A 10 7 4   ♣ 7 6 5
(b)   ♠ K J 8 7 2   ♡ 5   ◇ J 10 8 3   ♣ 10 9 7

South should pass the double on hand (a), which is completely balanced. But on hand (b) she should go for the spade game.

Responding to three-level doubles and overcalls

Although in theory this should be simple—the technique is basically the same as in responding to an ordinary double or overcall—some women seem to have trouble because they are averse to making bold jump bids on scanty values. Example:

WEST	NORTH	EAST	SOUTH
3◇	double	pass	?

south holds: ♠ 7   ♡ K J 7 6 4   ◇ A 6 2   ♣ 9 8 4 3

Since North is expected to hold a 16-point minimum, it is up to South to jump all the way to four hearts. Even though this will sometimes go awry, you just have to bid that way. Suppose North holds something like this:

♠ A Q 8 2   ♡ A 5 3   ◇ 10 4   ♣ K Q 10 5

Having bravely entered the fray on only 16 points, North can hardly be expected to bid again if she receives a minimum three-heart response to the double. Yet the heart game is a fair bet.

Three-Bids—the Aftermath

Three-bids, like men, you may adore or deplore—but not ignore. Not even when, for better or worse, the bidding is over and you have bought the deal. If you can break the blockade of an enemy shutout opening and still land in a reasonable contract, you have a chance to make the three-bid work for you.

Based as it usually is on a seven-card suit, a three-opening automatically tips off the fact that the opener holds no more than six cards in the other three suits. So, simply follow the highly effective policy of playing the *partner* of the three-bidder to hold length in those three suits.

Example:

```
              ♠ A 9 5 4
              ♡ 10 8
              ◇ A 9 6 4
              ♣ 9 8 2
♠ Q 8 6      ┌─────────────┐      ♠ 3
♡ J 9        │   NORTH     │      ♡ A K 7 6 4 3 2
◇ Q 7 5 3    │ WEST   EAST │      ◇ 8 2
♣ K Q 7 4    │   SOUTH     │      ♣ J 10 5
              └─────────────┘
              ♠ K J 10 7 2
              ♡ Q 5
              ◇ K J 10
              ♣ A 6 3
```

EAST	SOUTH	WEST	NORTH
3 ♡	3 ♠	pass	4 ♠
pass	pass	pass	

West opens the jack of hearts. East wins the first two tricks, shifting to the jack of clubs, which South wins with the ace.

Had there been no opposition bidding, South would probably follow the normal percentage play in trumps, cashing out the ace and king and hoping to drop the queen—a play that mathematically has the edge on a finesse. After East's three-heart bid, however, South decides to play West to hold length in the other three suits, so she lays down the trump king and runs the jack on the second round.

As expected, West holds the trump queen, so South pulls a third round of trump and tackles diamonds, a suit in which she needs to win four tricks in order to have a parking place for a losing club. Still placing the unfortunate West with length in every suit but hearts, the "two-way" diamond finesse becomes strictly a one-way street: South cashes the diamond king and leads the jack, letting it ride if West does not cover. Thus South lands the game contract.

South had the odds going for her on both these vital finesses, because when she tackled trumps, she knew East held seven hearts, leaving only six empty slots in his hand. West, in contrast, was marked with two hearts and thus had *eleven* empty slots. Clearly the spade queen was more likely to be in the hand with eleven empty slots than the one with six.

By the time South got around to tackling diamonds, the odds in her favor had been trimmed a little, since West had shown up with three spades and East with only one. But by adding these figures to the hearts the defenders were known to hold, this still left West with eight vacant slots compared with East's five—sufficient reason to play West for the diamond queen. On a two-way finesse, 8 to 5 in your favor is a very profitable proposition.

On deals like this, you can often play with high accuracy by exploiting an enemy three-opening after the bidding is over. And sometimes the expectation of a favorable layout can enable you to *bid* high as well as play high. Here is an example to illustrate:

♠ A 5
♥ A 10 2
♦ A Q J 10 9
♣ 8 6 5

NORTH
SOUTH

♠ J 4 2
♥ K Q J 9 6 5
♦ 2
♣ A J 7

EAST	SOUTH	WEST	NORTH
3♠	4♥	pass	6♥
pass	pass	pass	

North has two reasons for shooting six hearts without checking whether South holds the club ace. The three-spade opening makes it likely that West will lead that suit, and therefore South might be able to wangle the slam even if the hand happened to be wide open in clubs. Furthermore, if South lacks the vital diamond king, that card is much more likely to be in West's hand than in East's, since East is marked with at least seven spades. This means South can probably take a winning diamond finesse if necessary.

In the world of the precarious preempt, this kind of measured boldness pays off.

Quizzes

QUIZ 1   What do you call in each of the following situations?

south holds: **the bidding:**

1 ♠ 6 2   **neither side vulnerable**
   ♡ K Q J 9 8 7 4 | SOUTH | WEST | NORTH | EAST |
   ◇ Q 10 9 | ? | | | |
   ♣ 4

2 ♠ J 4 3   **neither side vulnerable**
   ♡ 8 | EAST | SOUTH | WEST | NORTH |
   ◇ K 9 | pass | ? | | |
   ♣ K 10 7 5 4 3 2

3 ♠ Q J 7 6 5 3 2   **East-West vulnerable**
   ♡ 10 | NORTH | EAST | SOUTH | WEST |
   ◇ 7 | pass | pass | ? | |
   ♣ J 9 6 5

4 ♠ 3   **North-South vulnerable**
   ♡ K Q J 10 8 6 5 | NORTH | EAST | SOUTH | WEST |
   ◇ K J 7 2 | pass | pass | ? | |
   ♣ A

5 ♠ K 10 9 2   **both sides vulnerable**
   ♡ A Q 9 8 7 5 4 | WEST | NORTH | EAST | SOUTH |
   ◇ 8 | pass | pass | pass | ? |
   ♣ 10

Answers

1 *Three hearts.* With six probable tricks in hearts, plus a potentially valuable holding in diamonds, this would almost be worth four hearts if East-West were vulnerable. But at equal vulnerability, it does not pay to take too many chances, since opponents are apt to be quick on the trigger.

2 *Pass.* Clubs do not possess a high enough shutout value to justify taking risks. Furthermore, the suit is broken, and since East has already passed there is insufficient reason to take a journey into danger by opening three.

3 *Three spades.* In third position at favorable vulnerability, you can take chances—especially when you hold the tops-for-stopping-power spade suit.

4 *Four hearts.* Since partner has already passed, slam chances are slender, so we can cut corners by going direct to game. This will make it difficult for East-West to locate a cheap save.

5 *One heart.* Both opponents have already passed, so there is little chance they can outbid us. A three-heart bid would, in any case, be unwise since we hold four cards in the other major suit. A purist might cavil at a one-bid on only 9 high-card points, but it would be a grave error to pass up such a powerful distribution.

    QUIZ 2   Your partner has opened a preemptive bid. What do you call on each of the following hands?

south holds:			the bidding:			
1	♠ 8 6		**neither side vulnerable**			
	♡ J		NORTH	EAST	SOUTH	WEST
	◇ A K 8 6 5		3 ♡	pass	?	
	♣ A K 10 4 2					

	south holds:		the bidding:		

2 ♠ A 8 2

    ♡ 6 4

    ◇ A 10 7 2

    ♣ A 8 6 5

both sides vulnerable

NORTH	EAST	SOUTH	WEST
3♡	pass	?	

3 ♠ K 10 6 4

    ♡ Q J 9 5

    ◇ 8

    ♣ A Q 9 4

neither side vulnerable

NORTH	EAST	SOUTH	WEST
3◇	pass	?	

4 ♠ Q 10 8 3

    ♡ 7 4

    ◇ A K J 5 2

    ♣ 9 2

neither side vulnerable

NORTH	EAST	SOUTH	WEST
3♣	3♠	?	

5 ♠ K J 7 3

    ♡ J 8 4 2

    ◇ 9 5 4

    ♣ 5 3

East-West vulnerable

SOUTH	WEST	NORTH	EAST
pass	pass	3♡	double
?			

Answers

1 *Four hearts.* Game will be touch-and-go, since North will doubt-less lose two spade tricks and must therefore limit trump losses to one. But North should hold a seven-card suit with only two gaps, so our singleton jack may be sufficient assistance.

2 *Four hearts.* This time we are on firm ground; our vulnerable partner should hold seven tricks to add to our three aces. Further-more, our two small trumps are adequate support for a trump suit that should have only one hole in it.

3 *Pass.* North has chosen a bad moment to open three, because it is unlikely the opponents could have made anything. But a bid of three notrump would merely make matters worse.

4 *Pass.* South should do nothing to incite West to bid a new suit, since East-West surely have a playable contract in hearts.

5 *Four hearts.* Or even *five* hearts. As partner is expected to be weak on defense, the opponents can certainly make game if not slam. It is up to us to keep up the good work that partner has initiated.

QUIZ *3*   Your opponents have opened a preemptive bid. What do you call in each of the following situations?

south holds: **the bidding:**

1   ♠ K J 2   neither side vulnerable

    ♡ A J 10 7 4

EAST	SOUTH	WEST	NORTH
3 ◇	?		

    ◇ 7

    ♣ A J 5 2

2   ♠ A K 3 2   both sides vulnerable

    ♡ 8 5

NORTH	EAST	SOUTH	WEST
pass	3 ♠	?	

    ◇ J 6 4 3

    ♣ A K J

3   ♠ K Q 10 9 2   North-South vulnerable

    ♡ 8

WEST	NORTH	EAST	SOUTH
3 ♣	pass	pass	?

    ◇ Q 10 7 2

    ♣ A 6 3

4   ♠ J 8   both sides vulnerable

    ♡ K J 6 5 4 2

WEST	NORTH	EAST	SOUTH
3 ♣	double	pass	?

    ◇ K 6 3

    ♣ 7 4

south holds:			the bidding:		
5	♠ Q J 2		neither side vulnerable		
	♡ 8 4 3		WEST	NORTH	EAST	SOUTH
	◇ A 5 4		3♠	double	pass	?
	♣ 9 8 6 5				

Answers

1 *Double.* 16 points is enough for a takeout double of a three-opening. (Three points more than are needed for a double of a one-bid.) With a hand that holds chances for game in either major suit, the double is better than bidding three hearts, which would suggest a one-suited hand.

2 *Pass.* Even if we wanted it to, a double would not stick, since partner would read it as a takeout request. We do not hold enough points for a bid of three notrump; and, finally, partner has already passed, which means that the chance to make game is slim.

3 *Three spades.* In fourth position you can bid on the same strength hand—normally 13 points—that would suffice for a one-level bid. And with a shortage in hearts, three spades is better than a takeout double.

4 *Four hearts.* Partner should hold 16 points on her takeout double and we hold 10—enough for game.

5 *Pass.* Although the double is for takeout, a bid of four clubs—our only suit—is far from attractive. Since we hold two sure defensive tricks, we should be able to pick up a sizable number by converting the double to a penalty double. Score consolation marks for a bid of three notrump.

Bee Gale Schenken

World's winningest woman in rubber bridge

Outstanding as her record is in national and international tournament competition, family comes first with Bee Schenken. After family and bridge she divides her time among culinary, art and charitable projects. The most remarkable aspect of her meteoric rise in bridge is that she did not win a national tournament until after her fortieth birthday. In fact, Bee's tournament debut did not take place until 1956; but in the next ten years she captured just about everything in sight, including the until-then lifelong bachelor, Howard Schenken, considered by many to be world's greatest player.

Unlike most of her fellow-woman experts, Bee actually prefers rubber bridge—an arena in which her percipience-plus-skill make her so outstanding that when Howard Schenken was asked to rank the leading female bridge players he said with pardonable pride, "I rank Bee among the first *one*."

Sometimes Bee is as impulsive at the bridge table as she is away from it, sensing when to be daring and when to be meek. Precisely because she is far from a coldly machine-like player, she personifies the ideal mentor to advise you on how to develop something resembling her own matchless flair for doing the right thing at the right time.

Female Intuition: What's It Worth?

Men call it "table presence"—and women don't make the most of it ... by Bee Gale Schenken

Ever since Queen Boadicea fastened long knives to her chariot wheels before leading her people in a desperate charge against the Roman invaders of ancient Britain, women have been looking for ways to tip the scales in our favor in the struggle against the supposedly dominant male. I am happy to admit—nay, boast—that my husband, Howard Schenken, is the greatest bridge player in the world. But the one thing he hasn't got is feminine intuition.

Instead, he has something called "table presence"—a keen awareness of and sensitivity to what goes on at the table. This quality is possessed only by the greatest of players: men players, that is. Our feminine intuition is so much like their table presence that it gives us a built-in advantage over all but the most percipient males. *If* we learn to use it wisely.

Once upon a time, a Little Old Lady stole a vulnerable game via a bluff opening bid. "She had a bag full of knitting," complained the victim to his teammates. "How could I tell she was going to psych bid?" How, indeed? But maybe *she* could tell that her opponent—a world champion and himself one of Europe's most celebrated bluff-bidders—was a better bet to psych against than a less high-powered player.

Sharpen up your intuition and you can rely on it to throw you a lifeline when pure technique is bound to fail. Even the most cold-blooded mathematician would agree that it is better to let a fifty-fifty decision be swung by table presence than by tossing a coin. And when it comes to salvaging a hopeless situation, table presence can help you find the only way. *Don't* look at the East-West cards in the following hand and see if you can find a hope of making the "impossible" spade slam.

```
                    ♠ J 10 5
                    ♡ A Q 9 5 3 2
                    ◇ 8
                    ♣ A 7 2
  ♠ K 9 4      ┌─────────────────┐      ♠ A 7
  ♡ 7 6        │     NORTH       │      ♡ 10 4
  ◇ Q J 9 7    │ WEST      EAST  │      ◇ 10 5 2
  ♣ K J 9 3    │     SOUTH       │      ♣ Q 10 8 6 5 4
               └─────────────────┘
                    ♠ Q 8 6 3 2
                    ♡ K J 8
                    ◇ A K 6 4 3
                    ♣ —
```

Having reached six spades, missing the ace and king of trumps, South won the club opening with dummy's ace and led the spade jack, which both defenders elected to duck. After this unexpected start—and with a slight hesitation by West to guide you—would your table presence be equal to the task of figuring out the exact spade layout, and profiting by it?

South decided that West, who obviously did not suspect East held the trump ace, had tried a cunning holdup with the king, doubtless hoping to cause entry trouble. If this were so, it might be possible to play on West's nerves by persuading him South held the ace and had seen through his little ruse. So instead of leading another trump from dummy, South entered the closed hand with a diamond and led a small spade away from the queen.

The result was gratifying. West decided that a wide-awake South had noticed the telltale hesitation on the first round of trump, and was now trying a blue-ribbon steal by craftily underleading the trump ace, hoping West would duck again. Determined not to be fooled, West went in with the king (his partner's ace of course falling on the same trick) and the slam came winging home.

If that can happen in a hotly-contested international match— as it did—then clearly there are many opportunities for the profitable use of table presence in this guileful game of bridge.

Hesitations and mannerisms, of course, provide the most prolific clues for players who possess table presence. Although it is unethical for a player to take notice of her *partner's* hesitations in bidding or play, it is perfectly legitimate to draw what inferences you can from your opponents' actions. Such inferences, however, are drawn entirely at one's own risk. Although there is a danger of being outwitted, there is no reason why one shouldn't play hunches provided there really is no better guide to the winning action. Just so you remember that bucking the percentages or deliberately making anti-systemic bids does not pay.

If you are sensitive to the real but elusive quality of table presence, you are likely also to be conscious of the fact that some players seem able to achieve a psychological ascendancy over certain opponents. Tournament players attach quite a lot of significance to this, sometimes to the extent of maneuvering for seats just so they can sit on the left of a player whom they regard as their special pigeon.

But even if you don't believe in Indian signs, it is important, in the highly-personalized combat of modern bridge, not to let a rival score a moral victory over you. In a women's team championship, the following deal gave me a big headache because a keen defender seemed well on the way to a resounding personal success that might have echoed in all our subsequent encounters.

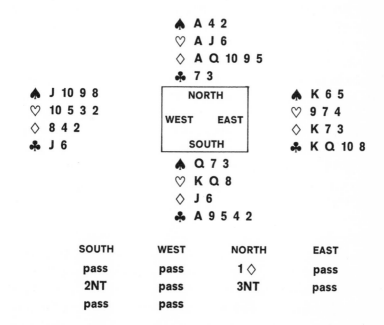

	NORTH	
	♠ A 4 2	
	♡ A J 6	
	◇ A Q 10 9 5	
	♣ 7 3	

WEST		EAST
♠ J 10 9 8		♠ K 6 5
♡ 10 5 3 2		♡ 9 7 4
◇ 8 4 2		◇ K 7 3
♣ J 6		♣ K Q 10 8

	SOUTH	
	♠ Q 7 3	
	♡ K Q 8	
	◇ J 6	
	♣ A 9 5 4 2	

SOUTH	WEST	NORTH	EAST
pass	pass	1 ◇	pass
2NT	pass	3NT	pass
pass	pass		

Sitting South, I received a spade opening lead from West. Had I known East held the spade king, I could have made sure of my contract by winning dummy's ace and tackling diamonds; but such a maneuver could have cost me the contract had West led from ♠ K J 10 x x, so I elected to play low. Having won the spade king, however, East shifted handily to the club eight. This was the only play to threaten me with the danger of defeat, since had East led the club king instead—as many players would have done—I could have won the ace and driven out the diamond king in complete safety. When East won the diamond she would have been unable to cash enough club tricks to defeat the contract, since the suit would have been blocked by West's jack and my ninespot would have provided a guard.

On East's actual return of the club eight, however, I had to duck the ace. West won the jack and returned a club, and I won the third round. I now had to decide whether to try the simple diamond finesse—a play which would, it so happens, have lost me the contract, since East would have amassed three club tricks as well as the diamond king and spade king.

The alternative was to attempt some kind of endplay against East, and since there happened to be a rather keen rivalry between us, I had a feeling that more depended on my decision than just this one contract. East's lead of the club eight on the second trick had been a sharp play that might not be reproduced when the deal was played at the other table. So if I flubbed the game East would score a personal triumph, which could have repercussions in the future.

But East's shrewdness proved to be a two-edged weapon. I calculated that she would not have found this play unless she happened to hold the diamond king. There was little rational basis for this decision, except that most defenders find it easier to produce tricky plays when they happen to hold the key cards. Since I had no other guide to the location of the diamond king this clue was sufficient. Besides, I sensed that East was tensed up, as though she were on the verge of a breakthrough—and this again suggested she held the diamond king. Finally, if East really did hold this vital card, I could see a way to cancel out her accurate defense.

Having won the club ace on the third round of that suit, I cashed out my winners in both major suits before exiting with a club, leaving East on play in this ending:

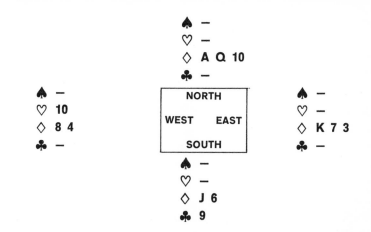

    Needing all the remaining tricks, I was sure to win them so long as East's last three cards were diamonds—as, of course, they were. On the return of the diamond trey by East, I put up the jack, knowing that if it held I could ditch dummy's last diamond loser on my winning club, while had West happened to produce the diamond king, dummy would have scooped the rest of the tricks.

    I'm still not sure whether a mathematician would endorse my line of play. But I do know that I feel pretty comfortable whenever I play against that particular East these days.

Table Presence in Doubling Situations

    Table presence is normally a separate department that merely serves to put a gloss on a player's basic technique. But sometimes table presence and technique blend so intimately that they are difficult to separate, and this is true in the field of doubles, rescues and bluff-bids. Of these, doubles are far the most important, psychologically as well as systemically, because X is not only the duplicate fan's abbreviation for a double: it also marks the spot where the temperature rises in *any* bridge game.

Most women are sound doublers in that we seldom attempt to harpoon our opponents in a makeable contract. But, more than men, we tend to miss profitable chances to double overcalls at a low level. This is probably because most of us wrongly assume that doubles of low contracts are too adventurous and aggressive.

Because most players do not overcall on strong hands—correctly preferring to double for takeout—most overcalls are made on less than 16 points. Since the partner of the overcaller must sometimes hold a poor or ill-fitting hand, this means that the moment of making an overcall is a moment of danger. Insubstantial overcalls are a necessary part of modern bridge because bidding is so highly competitive that anyone who never takes chances is too often robbed. Seasoned players shudder at weak overcalls, but they keep right on making them.

If you can blow the whistle at the psychological moment—when the overcaller's partner happens to be weak and the trump suit is breaking badly—you can win. By contrast, in a keen game there are few chances for fat doubles of high contracts, because the more bids that are made the more surely is a safe spot located. Hungry doublers, therefore, concentrate on overcalls, and the two key factors in doubling such a call are your trump holding and your holding in the suit partner has opened.

Your trump holding   It seldom pays to double a low-level overcall with less than four trumps, except at duplicate, where three may be enough if your opponents are vulnerable. Furthermore, the best trump trick to hold is not the ace, but an "unexpected" winner that will jar the overcaller's calculations out of joint. After an opening bid of one heart and an overcall of two clubs, which of the following hands would you rather double on?

(a) ♠ J 6 2   ♡ 10 7   ◇ K Q 9 2   ♣ A 5 4 2
(b) ♠ A 6 2   ♡ 10 7   ◇ K Q 9 2   ♣ J 10 4 3

Hand (a) is not a good double of two clubs, since it contains no "unexpected" trump tricks. The overcaller knew he did not hold the ace when he bid two clubs, so it is better to bid two diamonds instead of doubling.

Hand (b), however, is fine for a double of two clubs, even though it contains exactly the same number of high-card points. The "unexpected" trump trick makes the difference.

Holding five or more cards in your opponent's suit is not always quite such a soft touch as it might seem, since your partner is likely to be correspondingly short on trumps and you may therefore find it difficult to make a double stick. Sometimes it can even pay better to pass instead of doubling. Let us suppose partner opens one spade, there is an overcall of two hearts, and you hold:

♠ 8　♡ K J 9 5 3　◇ Q 10 4 2　♣ 10 9 3

There is a strong chance that partner holds a singleton or void heart, in which case she might remove a double to an unhealthy spade contract. It is therefore better to pass the two-heart overcall, hoping partner can double for takeout. This of course you would pass for penalty. But even if two hearts were passed out, the chances are you would score better this way than by doubling.

In a similar situation, however, you could double a two-heart overcall on the following hand:

♠ 10 2　♡ A Q 9 3 2　◇ A 9 7　♣ Q 9 2

Although it is not very likely partner will stand a double of two hearts, you can afford to double on the slender chance that she might stand it. The fact that you hold 12 high-card points makes the difference, since it means you can handle any situation that develops. On the previous hand, you did not hold enough points to handle the situation if partner removed the double.

Your holding in partner's suit   Since a low-level double is essentially a bargain-hunting operation, its efficacy does not depend entirely on how many tricks you can set your opponents. Equally important is how big a score your team could have gotten if you hadn't doubled. And both these factors are heavily influenced by the nature of your holding in the suit partner has opened.

If you hold strength in your partner's suit, a double is apt to disappoint; either the declarer or the dummy will be short in that suit and some of your team's high cards will not live to win tricks. Also, a strong holding in partner's suit makes it more likely you could have scored a game.

But if you are short in the suit partner has bid, her high cards in that suit are more likely to win tricks against the doubled contract—and you may also be able to score some ruffs. Furthermore, it is possible you and your partner hold misfit hands and could not have made game had you not doubled. In short, the best doubles are based on misfit hands. Example:

♠ 7 4   ♡ Q 10 8 2   ◇ A K J   ♣ 10 9 4 3

If partner opens the bidding and your opponent overcalls two clubs, the attractiveness of a double depends on which suit your partner has bid. Opposite a one-spade opening, a double of two clubs would be fine. But opposite a one-heart or one-diamond opening, the double should be rejected in favor of a raise of partner's suit.

For doubling purposes, the best holding in partner's suit is a singleton or a doubleton, since a void can be a handicap opposite a broken holding such as A Q 10 x or K J x x. But other pros and cons can affect these doubles. For example, opener has to be free to remove the double if her hand is unsuitable for defense play, and this means you should hold at least 8 high-card points before you can double any low-level overcall. These points are needed to make your hand playable in whatever spot partner selects, should she pull the double.

The vulnerability situation also counts heavily. As well as doubling readily when the opponents are vulnerable, it is wise to think twice when your own team is. A double when you are vulnerable means you may be trading a high-scoring vulnerable game for the penalty that you hope to collect. To be acceptable, this penalty has got to be bigger. Especially at duplicate, this factor can swing the decision. Example:

♠ K 10 2   ♡ 9 7 4 3   ◇ Q J 7   ♣ A J 5

Partner opens one diamond and, after an overcall of two clubs, you have to consider whether to double or bid two notrump. Against the double is the fact that you hold only three trumps and too much strength in partner's diamond suit; but the double would still be a fair speculation if the opponents were vulnerable and you were not. If, however, the vulnerability were the other way around, two notrump would be the recommended call.

Good doublers are also good psychologists. Risky with all strange partners, close doubles can be suicidal with a highly temperamental partner who is too easily put out of gear by disaster. With such a partner, you stand to lose too much if the double fails to work.

Finally, the player who has good table presence can make big unseen profits via her ability to react quickly in potential doubling situations. Slow or hesitant doubles can help the opposition by tipping off the doubler's hand at the same time as they hinder the opening bidder by imposing an ethical strain. Following is a very common situation.

SOUTH	WEST	NORTH	EAST
1 ♠	2 ♣	double	pass
?			

south holds: ♠ K Q J 5 3   ♡ A K J 2   ◇ 10 7   ♣ 6 3

Whether South should stand the double is a fairly moot point, but—given a free hand—South would probably elect to remove the double to two hearts.

If North hesitated before doubling, however, South would be under an ethical strain. This is because a player whose partner has hesitated is under the obligation not to take advantage of any information conveyed by that hesitation. If, therefore, North's double of two clubs was hesitant, a scrupulous South would probably leave the double in even though she would be pretty sure this was a losing decision. Honorable players would rather lose points than be suspected of an ethical violation.

A hesitant double, therefore, means that the doubler's partner is less free to pull the double on precisely those hands where it *ought* to be pulled. So penalty doubles, even more than other bids, should preferably be made after a measured few seconds' thought, thus avoiding either undue haste or undue reluctance.

This tip can help. It can also enhance your "intuition" status. If your opponent telegraphs an overcall via a warning huddle, start figuring immediately what action you will take over any call he may make. For example, suppose your partner opens one spade, the next player huddles, and you hold:

♠ K 6   ♡ A 8 5 3   ◇ J 7 2   ♣ J 10 6 4

A one-notrump overcall you can handle, since you hold enough high-card points for a penalty double. A two-diamond overcall would be no problem, since you lack sufficient trumps for a double.

So the most likely way you may be handed a headache is via an overcall of either two clubs or two hearts. This, then, is the problem you should address yourself to while your opponent is thinking.

Since you have a suitable trump holding, you can double a butt-in two clubs, which would be no disaster even if it were made. But over a butt-in of two hearts, it would be better to bid two spades, since you hold no unexpected trump trick and dare not risk doubling the opposition into game.

If your opponent hesitates long enough for you to figure all this out—and sometimes he will—you can take any necessary action in a normal rhythm, having given no tip-off that you were considering a double. If you pass, you may later be given an opportunity to double at a higher level.

This kind of advance figuring is extra work. But it marks the successful psychologist whose opponents, getting no free information, make more than the normal number of false moves.

On Removing a Double

Not too long ago, removing your partner's penalty double was a quixotic and dangerous act. A long penance in the wilderness was automatic if you took out a double that would have paid dividends; and even if your decision to remove the double was justified by events, you were hung with no garlands.

But times have changed, and for up-to-the-minute players a low-level penalty double is no longer a "hands off" order. Instead, a double is more in the nature of a good-natured suggestion: doubler's partner is expected to scan her hand critically, making sure her hand is suitable for defense play before she passes.

Arguments whether a double should or should not have been pulled probably cause more explosions and more busted partnerships than any other phase of the game. Yet oddly enough it isn't difficult to become a highly accurate judge of these situations.

The secret is to have in your mind a clear picture of what constitutes a sound minimum hand for leaving in a double, and only if your actual hand does not measure up to that minimum do you look around for an escape hatch.

The minimum hand for leaving in a double of an overcall is one with three defense tricks and two small trumps. Suppose you are South in the following situation:

SOUTH	WEST	NORTH	EAST
1 ♠	2 ♣	double	pass
?			

south holds: ♠ K Q 8 3   ♡ A K 7 2   ◇ J 8 6   ♣ 9 4

This is a typical minimum hand for leaving the double in, since you hold three defense tricks (the spade king-queen and the heart ace-king) plus two small trumps. If the hand were weaker in any material respect, you would be well advised to remove the double.

Once you know what a typical minimum "leave-in" hand looks like, you merely need to notice the fine points that can make a hand better or worse on defense.

The fine points of close doubles   Extra trumps are the key factor when you are considering leaving in a double on a doubtful hand. If you hold as many as three trumps, you can stand a double even if your hand is short on defense tricks. Example:

SOUTH	WEST	NORTH	EAST
1 ♡	2 ♣	double	pass
?			

south holds: ♠ Q J 7   ♡ K Q 10 9 2   ◇ 7 6   ♣ A 5 3

South holds only about two defense tricks, but she can let North's double stand because she has an extra club to compensate. Had West's overcall been two diamonds instead of two clubs, a removal to two hearts would be indicated because of the shortage of defense tricks and the lack of extra trumps.

Although an extra trump can compensate for a shortage of defense tricks, this process doesn't work too well in reverse. If you are short on the regulation two trumps, it is usually best to remove the double, even if you hold extra defense tricks, since the chances are you can score better by playing the deal yourself. Never stand a low-level double on a void trump, and seldom on a singleton.

A strong factor in standing a double is the presence of top cards—the ace, or ace and king—in the suit you have bid. Partner is likely to be short in that suit, having based her double partly on the expectation of scoring a ruff or two, and this dream is obviously more likely to come true if you hold top cards. This can swing the decision in a situation like the following:

SOUTH	WEST	NORTH	EAST
1 ♠	2 ◇	double	pass
?			

south holds: (a) ♠ A K 5 4 2 ♡ K 8 7 4 ◇ 6 3 ♣ K 6

(b) ♠ J 9 7 6 5 ♡ K Q J 2 ◇ 6 3 ♣ K Q

Hand (a) is a nice one on which to leave the double, since South holds an average defense hand with top cards in the suit she has bid.

Hand (b), by contrast, could disappoint on defense, since the expected spade opening lead could cost a trick, and South may not be able to hand partner any spade ruffs fast enough. A removal to two hearts is indicated.

If you hold a second suit that you have not bid, there is a danger partner may hold duplicating strength in that suit, in which case your defense tricks may be telescoped and a double may yield a disappointing penalty. This danger is so great that *one should hardly ever stand a double on a hand that contains an unbid five-card suit.* And even with only a four-card suit, keen judgment is needed for winning decisions.

SOUTH	WEST	NORTH	EAST
1♠	2♣	double	pass
?			

south holds: ♠ K J 7 6 3   ♡ Q 10   ◇ A K 8 7   ♣ 6 2

This is a pretty tough problem. South holds slightly less than three nailed-down defense tricks, and does not hold extra trump length to compensate. Furthermore, she has an unbid diamond suit, which may possibly clash with a diamond suit in North's hand and thus produce few defense tricks.

On the other hand, South's prospects of making game if she takes out the double are not too bright. North is expected to be short on spades, so it would be a mistake to rebid that suit, and it would be difficult to score an 11-trick game in diamonds. Therefore, since no takeout bid is attractive, South should stand the double.

Now suppose that the bidding is exactly the same but South holds a heart suit instead of a diamond suit, making her hand as follows:

♠ K J 7 6 3   ♡ A K 8 7   ◇ Q 10   ♣ 6 2

This time there is a slightly better chance to make game if South removes the double, since her unbid suit is a major instead

of a minor. This is enough to swing a knife-edge decision, so South
bids two hearts instead of standing pat.

Sometimes this kind of reasoning can be a morale-stiffener
when you are faced with an "impossible" problem. Consider
South's plight in the following sequence:

SOUTH	WEST	NORTH	EAST
1 ♠	2 ♦	double	pass
?			

south holds: ♠ J 6 5 3 2   ♡ A Q 2   ♦ 5   ♣ K J 10 8

With only two defense tricks and a singleton trump, one in-
stinctively recoils from the idea of leaving in the double. Unfortunately, there are snags in any takeout bid; the spade suit is too
weak to rebid, and it would be a mistake to bid three clubs—a high
reverse—on a minimum hand. South might wriggle off the hook
via a nervy bid of two hearts—but she might also land on a worse
one.

Of course it is South's own fault she is in this predicament:
Cinderella should have known she was going to have a problem
at midnight, and should therefore have opened one club, leaving
an easy rebid of one spade for the second round. But having got
into this scrape, my vote goes in favor of leaving in the double,
the reasoning being that the leave-in is the least of several available evils.

Notice that although we have considered this problem of
removing low-level doubles in considerable depth, I have said
nothing about the influence of vulnerability. This is because partner is expected to take this into account before doubling, and a
double should not be disturbed merely on the grounds that the
vulnerability is unfavorable.

SOUTH	WEST	NORTH	EAST
1 ♠	2 ♣	double	pass
?			

North-South only are vulnerable and

south holds: ♠ A Q J 3   ♡ K Q 9 3   ◇ A Q 7   ♣ 9 2

It is not uncommon to see a player leap into three notrump in this type of situation, arguing that an easy vulnerable game is likely to be worth more than a double against non-vulnerable opponents. But a South player who treats low doubles as a team operation will reflect that North knew all about the vulnerability situation when she doubled the two-club overcall, and will therefore respect that double. On South's fine hand, the penalty should be worth appreciably more than game.

Doubles of Game Contracts

There is so much avarice in the world that I am reluctant to add to it by putting too much emphasis on the profits that can be made via the penalty double. Nevertheless, it is my opinion that the ability to produce a shock double of a game contract—even when the opponents hold plenty of points for the bids they have made—is the hallmark of the truly formidable player. The advantage of pinning an intuitive double on your opponents is not merely that you thereby garner a bigger penalty. It also has a psychological effect on the opposition; when they play against you subsequently they will always be wondering whether the axe is about to descend. By contrast, these same players can afford to take liberties with players who have the reputation of never making a risky double.

Out-of-the-blue doubles need a sensitive ear and an ability to catch on fast when the cards seem to be lying badly for the declarer: in short, table presence. This attribute enabled West to score heavily for her team on the following deal:

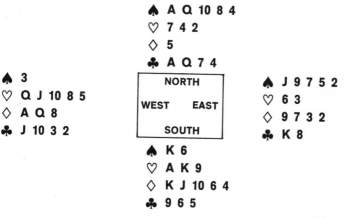

♠ A Q 10 8 4
♥ 7 4 2
♦ 5
♣ A Q 7 4

♠ 3
♥ Q J 10 8 5
♦ A Q 8
♣ J 10 3 2

♠ J 9 7 5 2
♥ 6 3
♦ 9 7 3 2
♣ K 8

♠ K 6
♥ A K 9
♦ K J 10 6 4
♣ 9 6 5

With both sides vulnerable, the bidding was:

SOUTH	WEST	NORTH	EAST
1 ♦	pass	1 ♠	pass
1NT	pass	2 ♣	pass
2 ♦	pass	2NT	pass
3NT	double	pass	pass
pass			

Even if you do not altogether approve the creepy-crawly North-South bidding, you have to concede that they held 26 high-card points, normally enough for game in notrump. Unfortunately, the East-West cards lay very badly, and on the automatic heart lead from West the declarer did well to collect seven tricks.

Neither North nor South was to blame for this setback, since

neither knew the missing cards were lying badly. But *West* knew—
and was quick-witted enough to turn a small prospective gain into
a 500 number. Holding the ace and queen of South's diamond
suit, West calculated she could establish her long hearts before
South could establish a single diamond trick. And since she herself held a singleton spade, West could reasonably gamble that
East would hold length in that suit, which would make it impossible for South to amass nine tricks in notrump without touching
diamonds. Furthermore, the gingerly North-South bidding had
made it evident that neither player held any extra points, so
there was no chance of a snappy redouble, nor of any overtricks
if West's calculations went awry.

As well as illustrating the thought processes of the successful
intuitive doubler, that deal supplies another useful tip. Had North
elected to raise straight to three notrump on the second round of
bidding, West would not have been able to double, since the risk
of finding North with a very powerful hand would have been too
great. Against opponents whom you know to be fast doublers,
therefore, it can be safer to bid boldly than to bid balkily.

The profits you can win via intuitive doubles do not end with
numbers on a score pad, because a well-timed double that scores
a hefty penalty will worry your opponents in future encounters.
They will tend to bid just that little bit less freely, and this can
alter the arithmetic of bridge in your favor. Did you ever consider that when a duplicate expert scores an "undeserved" top
because his opponents failed to bid high enough, he may have
earned that top via an out-of-the-blue double in an earlier clash
with that same pair of opponents?

Doubles, of course, can boomerang. Unless you possess tricks
that cannot melt away, it is prudent to assume that the declarer
will win one trick more if you double than he would have won had
you not doubled. This is because a double inevitably tips off the
declarer that bad breaks are around, and helps him place the

missing cards. But in the battle of wits between doublers and doublees, there is a shock tactic that can cancel out this tip-off and make it even more difficult for the declarer to plan the play in his doubled contract. This secret weapon is a double that is based on trumps in *your partner's* hand instead of your own. On the following deal, a special double of this type won West a shattering moral victory at the same time as it won her the board.

```
                    ♠ 10 4
                    ♡ K Q 10 3
                    ◇ J 10 7
                    ♣ Q 5 3 2
   ♠ A Q 9 6      ┌─────────────┐      ♠ 7 5 2
   ♡ 2            │    NORTH    │      ♡ J 7 6 4
   ◇ K 5 4 3 2    │ WEST   EAST │      ◇ 8 6
   ♣ 10 9 7       │    SOUTH    │      ♣ K J 8 4
                  └─────────────┘
                    ♠ K J 8 3
                    ♡ A 9 8 5
                    ◇ A Q 9
                    ♣ A 6
```

With both sides vulnerable, the bidding was:

SOUTH	WEST	NORTH	EAST
1NT	pass	2♣	pass
2♠	pass	2NT	pass
3♡	pass	4♡	pass
pass	double	pass	pass
pass			

Even though West held a powerful spade combination in back of South's spade bid, plus a probable diamond winner, many players would balk at doubling with only a singleton trump. But

West elected to double just *because* she held only a trump single-ton—a fact that told her East must hold four. (North would have bid a five-card heart suit had he held one, while South was marked by the bidding with exactly four hearts.) Because West's imaginative double was based on East's trump holding instead of her own, the declarer misread the trump situation and actually made fewer tricks than he might have made had he not been doubled. After West had opened the club ten, South had to lose two spade tricks, a diamond and a club, and he also lost a trump trick because he reasonably assumed that West held the missing jack. Thus East-West collected 500 points instead of the measly 100 that they might have picked up had West not doubled and had South taken a different position in the trump suit.

Imagine the traumatic effect of this kind of gambit! Next time South is doubled by that particular West, he won't feel safe to assume the double is a normal move, based on trump tricks in West's own hand. South will be unable to place the East-West cards with certainty—as one can when doubled by a conservative or unimaginative opponent—and therefore West is likely to snowball her successes.

Chances for imaginative doubles don't happen every day, but they are worth waiting for. In a situation like the following, a snappy double from West will win a victory that is more important than arithmetic.

SOUTH	WEST	NORTH	EAST
1 ◇	pass	2 ◇	pass
2 ♠	pass	3 ♠	pass
4 ♠	double	pass	pass
pass			

west holds: ♠ A   ♡ 9 7 6   ◇ A 7 5 3 2   ♣ 7 6 4 2

North-South should hold at least seven diamonds between them. West, after leading the diamond ace, can hand East a diamond ruff. After South gets back in, he again loses the lead to West via the spade ace, affording West the opportunity to lead to another diamond ruff. West downs the game contract at the same time she ups her moral ascendancy over the opponents.

When you make this type of double, the prospective penalty is not the only prize you are hoping to collect. The same is true of another defense weapon—the lead-directing double that is aimed more at promoting winning defense than inflicting penalties.

The Lead-Directing Double

If, as a defender, you could always hypnotize your partner into opening the suit you wanted, you would win decisively over most other players. This is because the fate of most contracts is settled on the opening lead. This is not because of the numerical value of the card led—most players make few mistakes there—but rather because of the suit led.

Telling partner the suit you want led   Unfortunately, there is no provision in the Laws of Bridge for hypnotic aids. But, against notrump contracts, there is nothing to stop you using a special double that tells partner the suit you want led: and although a lead-directing double seldom scores the big numbers that an ordinary penalty double can score, it really counts more. This is because a lead-directing double can defeat a contract that would otherwise have been made, and it thus saves the hidden game bonus in addition to scoring points for undertricks.

East called on a typical lead-directing double during the the following deal.

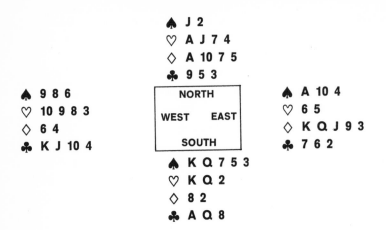

With both sides vulnerable, the bidding was:

SOUTH	WEST	NORTH	EAST
1♠	pass	2◇	pass
2NT	pass	3NT	double
pass	pass	pass	

In response to East's double, West opened a diamond and the contract was set just one trick—200 points—East winning four diamond tricks plus the spade ace. Had East not doubled for a diamond lead, West would probably have opened a heart or a club, and South would have made at least ten tricks for a score of 630. Thus the double made a difference of 830 points.

After any given bidding sequence, a double of three notrump by the player not on lead will pinpoint just one suit, so before you can double you have to know exactly what that suit is. Even regular expert partnerships have been known to have misunderstandings on this subject, and I recommend sticking closely to the following four-point plan.

1 *The doubler has bid a suit*   When the player not on lead

has bid a suit, a double from that player requests a lead of that suit. Example:

NORTH	EAST	SOUTH	WEST
1♣	1♠	1NT	pass
3NT	double	pass	pass
pass			

west holds: ♠ 5　♡ J 7 6 2　◊ Q J 10 9 4　♣ 9 5 4

Even though West holds a watertight sequence in diamonds, she must open her singleton spade in loyalty to East's double. East probably holds a spade suit with only one hole in it, plus a fast reentry.

2 *The doubler's partner has bid a suit*　In this case, the double suggests a lead of the suit that has been bid. Example:

WEST	NORTH	EAST	SOUTH
1♠	2♣	pass	2NT
pass	3NT	double	pass
pass	pass		

west holds: ♠ Q 9 4 3 2　♡ K Q 10　◊ K Q 7 5　♣ 7

Without the double, West might consider leading a diamond or heart, since if the North-South bidding is taken at face value a spade lead seems hopeless. East's double, however, confirms that a spade opening is desired—probably because East holds the vital king or jack.

3 *Dummy has bid one suit*　If neither defender has bid, but the dummy has bid one suit, a double calls for a lead of that suit.

4 *Dummy has bid two suits*　This can be a tough situation, and you may have to use judgment in deciding which of dummy's

two suits to open. For example, if you happen to hold long cards in one of dummy's suits, it is unlikely that your partner holds long cards too, so she probably wants the other suit led.

NORTH	EAST	SOUTH	WEST
1♠	pass	2♣	pass
2♡	pass	2NT	pass
3NT	double	pass	pass
pass			

west holds: ♠ 10 7   ♡ J 10 6 3 2   ◇ 8 6   ♣ J 9 7 4

Since West holds five cards in dummy's heart suit, it is highly unlikely that East can hold enough hearts to wish them led. West should therefore open the spade ten. As a general rule, in any situation where you have no clue which of dummy's two suits your partner wants you to lead, you should lead the first-bid suit.

When you double for a lead, you don't necessarily have to be able to wreck the contract all by yourself. Sometimes it is a fair gamble to double even though you are not quite certain where the setting tricks are coming from—provided you can gauge from the bidding that the opponents do not hold enough points to redouble. Would you say that East could afford to double in the following situations?

SOUTH	WEST	NORTH	EAST
pass	pass	1◇	pass
1NT	pass	2♣	pass
2♡	pass	2NT	pass
3NT	pass	pass	?

east holds: ♠ 5 4   ♡ 7 4 2   ◇ Q J 10 8 2   ♣ A Q 6

East cannot be certain of beating three notrump unless West can deliver one or two high cards, but the bidding has made it pretty clear that West is likely to hold those cards. (North-South have limped into the three-notrump contract after South has passed initially. Furthermore, North was not strong enough to jump the bidding on the second round.) Therefore it is a fair gamble to double for a diamond lead—dummy's first-bid suit.

NORTH	EAST	SOUTH	WEST
1♠	pass	2NT	pass
3NT	?		

east holds: ♠ A Q 10 8 ♡ A 8 4 ◇ J 7 3 ♣ 10 9 5

This time it would be highly dangerous to double for a spade lead, since there is no reason why West should hold any points at all. In this case, a spade lead would merely hold the declarer to one overtrick, redoubled.

You've probably noticed that all these examples have been doubles of notrump. Unfortunately, *you cannot double a suit contract for a lead. All doubles of suit contracts below slam are regular penalty doubles.* But such a double can nevertheless yield a small clue, since the doubler will frequently hold strength in dummy's suit. This can influence your choice of lead. Example:

NORTH	EAST	SOUTH	WEST
1♡	pass	1♠	pass
1NT	pass	2◇	pass
2♠	pass	3♠	pass
4♠	double	pass	pass
pass			

west holds: ♠ A 10 3 ♡ 10 6 ◇ 9 7 6 ♣ Q 9 5 3 2

East's penalty double may be based partly on the unconvincing way the bidding has unwound, but she could hardly have risked the double unless she held tricks in dummy's heart suit. And since West holds ruffing potential in that suit, plus a fast trump trick, the ten of hearts is the opening.

The Slam Double

Since experienced players will seldom go down more than one trick in slam, it is not worth doubling them for the size of the penalty. Therefore one can use the slam double to pinpoint a special opening lead. And—unlike lead-directing doubles of lesser contracts—these doubles can be made against suit slams just as well as notrump slams.

The special opening that a slam double invites is simply an *unusual* one. Of course, if you think that a normal lead from partner is likely to prove the winning one, or if you think no lead is likely to wreck the slam, you do not double.

What constitutes an "unusual" lead? This depends on the bidding, but obviously a suit that has been bid by either defender is *not* unusual, nor is a trump. And if neither defender has bid, the lead of an unbid suit would not be unusual either. Via a process of elimination, therefore, you can usually figure out exactly which suit your partner wants you to lead. See if you can find West's winning opening in the following situations.

SOUTH	WEST	NORTH	EAST
1 ♡	pass	2 ♣	pass
3 ♡	pass	4NT	pass
5 ♡	pass	6 ♡	double
pass	pass	pass	

west holds: ♠ K 7 5 3   ♡ 6 3   ◇ J 8   ♣ 9 7 6 5 2

West should lead a club. Neither a spade nor a diamond would be "unusual," since West would normally lead an unbid suit had East not doubled. And since a trump lead is never unusual, the only suit left is clubs. It is likely that East is void of clubs and hopes to win a free trick on the opening lead.

NORTH	EAST	SOUTH	WEST
1 ◇	pass	1 ♡	pass
2 ♣	pass	3 ♡	pass
4NT	pass	5 ♡	pass
6 ♡	double	pass	pass
pass			

west holds: ♠ J 10 9 5 3 ♡ 9 4 ◇ 8 7 5 ♣ 9 3 2

West should lead a diamond. The double warns West against opening the unbid spade suit, which would be the normal lead without a double. When dummy has bid two suits it is correct to lead the first suit unless there is some clue to the contrary.

NORTH	EAST	SOUTH	WEST
1NT	2 ◇	3 ♠	pass
4 ♠	pass	4NT	pass
5 ♡	pass	6 ♠	pass
pass	double	pass	pass
pass			

west holds: ♠ 6 3 2 ♡ 9 6 4 3 2 ◇ J 8 ♣ 9 8 5

West should lead a club. The double clearly excludes a diamond or a trump opening, so the choice is between clubs and hearts. It could be legitimate for East to double in this situation even if she knew West would be faced with a blind guess between these two suits, but had East wanted a heart opening against the slam, she could have doubled the Blackwood bid of five hearts; since she did not, it is right to assume that a club is desired.

As you see, it usually isn't difficult to figure out which lead a slam double invites. Tougher than the problem of locating the winning lead, actually, is the problem of gauging exactly when to double. This needs a fast, smooth decision. It can be misleading, or even unethical, to hesitate and pass. When your opponents are heading for slam, it is likely you have been passing rhythmically; if you suddenly pause to consider whether to double, that pause will be as inconspicuous as an ink blob on a bridal gown.

There is only one answer—table presence. You have to keep on the ball, and figure out what action to take *before* a critical situation arises. Imagine that you are West in the following situation and see whether you can do all your thinking in advance.

WEST	NORTH	EAST	SOUTH
pass	1 ◇	pass	2 ♡
pass	3 ◇	pass	4 ◇
pass	4NT	pass	5 ◇
pass	6 ◇	pass	pass
?			

west holds: ♠ A 9 8 2   ♡ 10 8 6 4 2   ◇ 8 7 5 4   ♣ —

Although West badly wants a club opening, she should pass the six-diamond bid, since a double would not produce the desired result. Here the only "unusual" opening lead would be a heart—dummy's suit—and a heart opening would be automatic if West doubled. By contrast, if West passes, East can infer that a normal lead of an unbid suit is required, and there is a fifty-fifty chance she will come up with the winning club opening. Especially if she relies on that much-undervalued asset—feminine intuition.

Quizzes

QUIZ 1 In the following situations, South has to consider whether to double for penalties at a low level. No vulnerability.

south holds: **the bidding:**

1 ♠ 8 7 5

♡ K Q 10

◇ A K 4 2

♣ 10 8 6

NORTH	EAST	SOUTH	WEST
1 ♡	2 ◇	?	

2 ♠ 6 4

♡ A J 8 3

◇ Q 10 8 2

♣ 10 9 7

NORTH	EAST	SOUTH	WEST
1 ♠	2 ◇	?	

3 ♠ A 10 5

♡ A 10 9 3 2

◇ K 10 6 3

♣ J

SOUTH	WEST	NORTH	EAST
1 ♡	pass	2 ♣	2 ◇
?			

4 ♠ A K 8 7

♡ J 5

◇ J 6 2

♣ 10 6 3 2

WEST	NORTH	EAST	SOUTH
1 ♠	double	2 ♣	?

5 ♠ 2

♡ 10 9 4

◇ K Q 10 5 3

♣ Q 6 3 2

NORTH	EAST	SOUTH	WEST
1 ♠	2 ◇	?	

Answers

1 *Three hearts.* South holds too much strength in her partner's heart suit for a double to be attractive. Also, she holds no "unexpected" tricks in East's diamond suit; East probably holds ◊ Q J 10 9 x x and is fully prepared to lose the ace and king.

2 *Double.* This time the trump holding is ideal, since East is probably slated to lose two more trump tricks than she expected. Notice that the nature of the trump holding is more important than the general strength of the hand.

3 *Double.* Although South has opened on a minimum hand, the double is very good, since she holds a singleton in North's suit.

4 *Double.* The reason for doubling on such a poor club holding is that North is expected to hold some clubs—as well as some diamonds and hearts—on the takeout double of one spade. It is hard for South to show that she holds a few points if she doesn't double.

5 *Pass.* There is a danger that North might remove a double into a distasteful spade contract. The best chance of a plus is that North will either double two diamonds for takeout or pass.

QUIZ 2   Your partner has made a low-level penalty double. What call do you make? Both sides vulnerable.

south holds:

the bidding

1	♠ A K 7 2	SOUTH	WEST	NORTH	EAST
	♡ A 10 9 3	1 ♠	2 ◊	double	pass
	◊ 10 6	?			
	♣ Q 5 3				

2	♠ Q 8 7 3 2	SOUTH	WEST	NORTH	EAST
	♡ A K J 9	1 ♠	2 ♣	double	pass
	◊ A Q 7	?			
	♣ 9				

south holds: **the bidding:**

3	♠ J 2	**SOUTH**	**WEST**	**NORTH**	**EAST**
	♡ K J 9 7	1 ♡	2 ♣	double	pass
	◇ K J 8 2	?			
	♣ A 5 3				

4	♠ J 9 7 5 3	**SOUTH**	**WEST**	**SOUTH**	**EAST**
	♡ A J 7 2	1 ♠	1 NT	double	pass
	◇ K 8	?			
	♣ A 5				

5	♠ K 9 8	**NORTH**	**EAST**	**SOUTH**	**WEST**
	♡ A 10 7	1 ♠	pass	2 ♣	2 ◇
	◇ 5	double	pass	?	
	♣ Q 10 6 5 3 2				

Answers

1 *Pass.* With three defense tricks and two trumps, this is a minimum, but eminently acceptable, hand for leaving in partner's double.

2 *Two hearts.* Although the hand is strong on high-card points, three factors argue against leaving in the double. South holds only a singleton trump, she has a fine major suit that she has not yet shown, and she is far from certain that an opening lead in the suit she has bid (spades) will prove beneficial.

3 *Pass.* Although South is not certain she can deliver three defensive tricks, she holds an extra trump to compensate. Furthermore, the ace of trumps is especially valuable when partner has doubled at a low level since it means that between you you will almost certainly control the trump suit.

4 *Pass.* When partner doubles an overcall of notrump, you should not, in principle, remove the double, even if you hold a minimum hand. The only time you might consider a takeout is when your

hand is extremely unbalanced and it seems that a bigger score can be made in a trump contract than on defense.

5 *Two spades.* When removing a double, the attractiveness of the contract that you are removing to is always a factor in the decision. In this instance a spade contract looks very good, since your hand should be worth a couple of ruffing tricks.

QUIZ 3 In some, but not all, of the following situations, there is a chance to make a lead-directing double. What call do you make? Both sides vulnerable.

south holds:

the bidding:

1

♠ 6 5 3
♡ K Q J 10 3
◇ A 7
♣ A 8 6

SOUTH	WEST	NORTH	EAST
1 ♡	pass	pass	1 ♠
pass	2 NT	pass	3 NT
?			

2

♠ 5 2
♡ 10 9 4 2
◇ K Q 10 8
♣ J 9 8

EAST	SOUTH	WEST	NORTH
1 ◇	pass	1 ♡	1 ♠
pass	pass	2 NT	pass
3 NT	?		

3

♠ 10 7 3 2
♡ K 10 5
◇ 6 4
♣ 10 9 4 2

NORTH	EAST	SOUTH	WEST
1 ♡	1 ♠	pass	1 NT
pass	2 NT	pass	3 NT
pass	pass	?	

4

♠ Q 10 3
♡ 5 3
◇ 7 6 4
♣ A Q J 10 2

EAST	SOUTH	WEST	NORTH
1 ♣	pass	1 ♡	pass
1 ♠	pass	2 NT	pass
3 NT	?		

south holds:		the bidding:		
		WEST	NORTH	EAST	SOUTH

5 ♠ J 10 5 3 2
♡ J
◇ A 6
♣ K Q J 8 2

WEST	NORTH	EAST	SOUTH
1 ♠	pass	2 ◇	pass
2 ♡	pass	2 ♠	pass
2 NT	pass	3 NT	?

Answers

1 *Double.* When you or your partner have bid a suit, a double of notrump asks for that suit to be led. Since you are certain to defeat the contract on a heart opening, you should double; otherwise, partner may take too much notice of the opponents' bidding and try one of the unbid suits.

2 *Pass.* A diamond opening would probably be very enjoyable, but unfortunately a double in this situation asks for a lead of partner's suit, not dummy's.

3 *Double.* Although you are not altogether certain to defeat the contract, you must make quite sure partner leads a heart. If you pass, there is a chance that she may try to find you in one of the other suits. Notice that although you do not hold much in the way of high cards, the double is the marked call, for there is no fear of a redouble. The opponents cannot possibly have enough points for that.

4 *Double.* When neither you nor your partner has bid, a double asks for a lead of dummy's suit; and when dummy has bid two suits, the double asks for the first-bid suit. The underlying theory is simple: if you hold strength in dummy's *second* suit, you might have bid it yourself.

5 *Pass.* E-W are probably in too ambitious a contract, but a double would ask for a lead of dummy's diamond suit. If you pass quietly, partner will probably lead a club even if she is short in that suit, since she will realize that it is important to set up your hand.

QUIZ 4   Your partner has doubled an enemy slam contract, asking for an unusual opening. Which card do you lead?

south holds: **the bidding:**

1	♠ 5		WEST	NORTH	EAST	SOUTH
	♡ Q 10 9 7 3 2		1◇	pass	1♠	pass
	◇ 8 4		2♣	pass	3♠	pass
	♣ J 7 6 2		4 NT	pass	5◇	pass
			6♠	double	all pass	

2	♠ 8 5		WEST	NORTH	EAST	SOUTH
	♡ 9 2		1 NT	4♣	6♠	pass
	◇ J 9 6 5 4 3 2		pass	double	all pass	
	♣ 9 6					

3	♠ 10 7 3 2		EAST	SOUTH	WEST	NORTH
	♡ J 6 4		1◇	pass	1♡	pass
	◇ 8 2		3 NT	pass	6 NT	double
	♣ J 7 5 3		all pass			

4	♠ 10 9 7		EAST	SOUTH	WEST	NORTH
	♡ A Q J 10 5 2		1♣	1♡	3♣	3♡
	◇ 9 6 4		4♣	pass	4◇	pass
	♣ 2		6♣	pass	pass	double
			all pass			

5	♠ 9 8 6		EAST	SOUTH	WEST	NORTH
	♡ 10 7 6 5 3 2		1♣	pass	3♣	3♠
	◇ J 5 4		4 NT	pass	5◇	pass
	♣ 8		6♣	pass	pass	double
			all pass			

Answers

1 *Diamond eight*. North's double excludes a lead of the unbid

heart suit. A common meaning of the slam double is to ask for a lead of dummy's suit, and when dummy has bid two suits it is usually correct to lead the first.

2 *Diamond five.* It is a sure thing North does not want a club lead, since that would have been a normal lead without the double. As between hearts and diamonds, North evidently expects you to do some detective work. When made by a player who has pre-empted, this slam double often suggests a void suit, and since South holds seven diamonds it is more than likely that North is void of that suit.

3 *Heart jack.* Neither a club nor a spade would be "unusual," so North clearly wants a red-suit lead. A lead of dummy's suit is more likely to be required than the declarer's, and there may be an advantage in leading the jack since North may hold A Q 10.

4 *Spade ten.* The double eliminates a heart opening, since this would be the normal lead without the double. In choosing between spades and diamonds the clue is that West's four-diamond call was an ace-showing cue-bid, and North could easily have doubled then and there had she wanted a diamond opening. The inference, therefore, is that North wants a lead of the only remaining side suit, spades. South should resist the temptation to lay down the heart ace, since it may be ruffed.

5 *Heart five.* This is quite tricky, for although North's double clearly warns against the normal lead of the suit she has bid—spades—it seems that there is no clue to which of the red suits is required. The answer lies in West's Blackwood response of five diamonds. South must assume that North would have doubled that call had she wanted a diamond lead.

Helen Sobel Smith

Holder of largest number of national championships

No woman—and very few men—can match the thirty-three national championships won by Helen Sobel Smith, the seemingly fragile blonde who has been given the highest accolade of the opposite sex: she plays like a man. Helen agrees, but adds that her immense success is also due to the fact that she plays like a woman. By 1937, when she had been in tournament bridge only a year, her fame had become international.

Charles Goren chose her as the partner with whom he won the lion's share of the victories that helped to make him **Mr. Bridge**. With Goren, she twice won the Life Masters' Pairs, twice played on teams representing the United States in World Championships and won the International Pairs Competition played in London in 1957. Once, when a gushing Goren fan asked her, "How does it feel to play with a great expert?" she nodded across the table at Charlie and said, "Ask him." If you did ask him, he'd say without hesitation that she is not only the greatest woman player in the world but the greatest partner.

Her tournament wins include many with partners other than Goren. For years she shunned women's pair events—not because she didn't like playing with another woman, but because she felt that women didn't have to be coddled by keeping males away. To prove this beyond any doubt, she twice won the Open Pairs with Margaret Wagar—a feat that no other pair of women has ever accomplished.

How to Play Bridge with a Man

Partnering a man—some little-known facts on how experts think on defense . . . by Helen Sobel Smith

Men are my favorite partners. They are also my favorite opponents. I like a tough game and, at the top level of competition, I think men as a class play better than women. If this be treason, make the most of it. Let me show you how to do just that.

First, let's see why I think this. Well, men have greater physical stamina, for one thing. That's important in tournaments, where play runs nine days and world championship battles go on for close to two weeks.

Men appear to have greater powers of concentration. I say "appear to have" because I don't really believe that they *can* concentrate any better; it's just that they do. Few women are willing to stop thinking of family, clothes, beauty, appearance, men and other interests in order to bend every effort toward excelling at a game. A man is quite willing to partner a fellow he doesn't even like; he'll return your lead even if you just burned his house down—provided he is satisfied that this is the best percentage play he can make. But he will not return his best friend's lead or his boss's lead or his sweetheart's lead if he thinks he has figured out a better plan. And he expects his partner to do likewise, even when his partner is a woman.

But a woman—let's face it—may refuse to return partner's lead if she happens to be annoyed with her partner. Or she may return his lead out of love and loyalty even when she knows darn well there's a better play available.

Men don't expect this and don't understand it. So if you are going to play with a man, you will do well to try to adopt his single-minded pursuit of the best percentage chance and accomodate yourself to his way of thinking.

An illustration of this difference between men and women is shown by the following deal, which Charles Goren and I defended in a team game.

```
                    ♠ 10 9 4
                    ♡ 7
                    ◇ A J 10 8 3 2
                    ♣ Q 9 2
   ♠ A 8 5        ┌─────────────────┐      ♠ Q J 6 3 2
   ♡ Q J 10 8 4   │     NORTH       │      ♡ 6 3 2
   ◇ 5 4          │ WEST     EAST   │      ◇ K 6
   ♣ 10 4 3       │     SOUTH       │      ♣ K 8 5
                  └─────────────────┘
                    ♠ K 7
                    ♡ A K 9 5
                    ◇ Q 9 7
                    ♣ A J 7 6
```

SOUTH	NORTH
1NT	2NT
3NT	pass

I opened the heart queen from the West hand and, having won the trick with the ace, South led the diamond nine and let it ride. When Charlie won the king he had to decide whether to return my heart lead or shift to a spade.

The problem could have been solved by almost any experienced defender who took time out to figure South's points, but somewhere along the line quite a lot of women would allow themselves to be dissuaded from making the winning return. Consider first of all the woman who allows a misplaced sense of loyalty to override logic: she will argue that, on the one-notrump opening, South is almost certain to hold a spade stop and she will therefore persuade herself that there can't be any profit in returning a spade instead of a heart. Since this type of East player always *wanted* to return her partner's suit anyway, she will fire back a heart and South will make game via five diamond tricks, two hearts and the winning club finesse.

A strong-minded female defender will find reason for a better play. When South wins the opening lead with the ace of hearts, East will make a mental note that he holds the king as well—and since she can readily see that dummy is slated for five diamond winners, this East player will reason that if South happens to hold both the club ace and the spade ace, nine tricks are virtually already in the security box. The defense must therefore be predicated on the assumption that West holds one of the black aces. Furthermore, if West holds the *club* ace South must inevitably hold the spade ace *and king* in order to deliver the number of *points* needed for a standard notrump opening—and in this event South has again got nine fast tricks. Women who reason along these lines will therefore realize that there is no hope unless West holds the *spade* ace which will give the defenders a chance to run enough spade tricks to beat the hand.

Unfortunately, having worried their way through this very fine analysis, some women will flub the final test because their nerve will fail and they will return the *wrong* spade—the queen. South will cover with the king, and dummy's tenspot will stop the defenders running the suit.

This lead of the spade queen is a very natural-looking play and it therefore appeals to women much more than a "risky" underlead of the queen-jack sequence. But the underlead is the only play that has a chance to win, as my partner proved. After he had won the diamond king, Charlie led a small spade; and when South put on the king with a fatalistic air we ran off the entire spade suit, setting the contract two tricks.

Charlie had figured that to beat the contract West not only had to hold the spade ace; she had to hold two small spades as well, leaving South with specifically the doubleton king. This reasoning was 100 percent correct, since if South holds king-third of spades he can make absolutely certain of a spade stopper. (With ♠ K x x, South plays low from his hand if East leads a small spade, but covers with the king if East leads an honor.) On his actual spade holding, however, South was sure to rise with the king when East led a small spade, since it would be a mistake to play low if South had led away from the ace.

A perfect partner, Charlie will generously sugar-coat any pills that he has to hand out, and the only reason he ever raps his partners' knuckles is to make sure they stay awake for the next deal. Yet in the days when we regularly haunted the tournament trail, the traffic in ideas between us was very much a two-way affair. Charlie was well aware that half the world's bridge players are women, and he profited from the experience of feminine psychology that he got from our numerous post mortems, which usually took place in transit from one tournament to the next one.

Which brings me to my first precept on how to play with a man: Charlie and I seldom post-mortemed deals while actually at the card table—except when our opponents initiated a discussion —and I feel that such a policy is a judicious one for mixed partnerships. Men usually abound in sweet reasonableness when they are handing out advice, but they have a tendency to be slightly less rational when it comes to taking it themselves; and since in quite a number of mixed partnerships the female of the species is defter than the male, the best way to preserve masculine self esteem is to save the inquests until after the game.

My personal view of the problem of how to play with a man is that it is very much the same as the problem of how to defend *like* a man—and this is the theme on which my chapter is based largely.

As an introduction to this theme, I would like to emphasize an aspect of Goren point-count which too many players ignore.

Because I am what is known as a natural player, I have been misquoted as saying, "Points, schmointz, as long as you know what you're doing."

It is true that even before Charles Goren offered his point-count guide, I, as well as a limited group of experienced experts, could estimate the value of my hand and the probable value of the other hands around the table. Before point count, the process by which this was accomplished was about as easy to explain to the average player as Einstein's Theory. Nowadays, point count is the expert's short-cut key to his own methods—easier than thinking and for the most part just as accurate. In fact, in defense, it can be sensationally accurate, as you will soon see.

Defense—Active or Passive?

Inquisitive declarers often tote up dummy's points and make a mental note as to whether dummy has overbid or not. This is a harmless little habit, even if it doesn't help the declarer to play the hand any better; but for *defenders,* the same habit is a vital first line of defense.

A countdown on dummy's points can be your personal early warning system, alerting you to the scale of defense operation that is needed. By figuring how many points dummy *ought* to have for the bids he has made, and comparing this with the number of points dummy actually delivers, you can get some idea of your chances of beating the contract. If dummy is short on points, a maximum defense effort is likely to pay off: but if dummy seems to have several points to spare, then it is less likely that you can beat the hand and there may be little advantage in giving yourself a big headache.

NORTH	SOUTH
1 ◇	1 ♠
2NT	3 ♡
3 ♠	4 ♠
pass	

North puts down the following dummy:

♠ K Q J   ♡ 10 8 3   ◇ K J 5 4 2   ♣ A K

On his two-notrump rebid North ought to hold about 19 or 20 high-card points, but he actually holds only 17. Furthermore, although North holds strong trump support this is unlikely to count very heavily; South too is likely to hold strong spades. But North is very weak in the important heart suit. A maximum defense effort is justified.

NORTH	SOUTH
1 ♣	1 ♡
2 ♡	4 ♡
pass	

North puts down the following dummy:

♠ A 10   ♡ 10 9 7 2   ◇ A 10 9   ♣ A K J 4

This time North has failed to bid the full value of his hand; with 17 points he was well worth a raise to three hearts on the second round. Yet despite North's cautious two-heart rebid, South has bounced all the way to game without even taking the trouble to make a probing bid en route. The contract should be ironclad, and unless you happen to be endowed with unlimited stamina this deal is unlikely to be worth a very large investment of mental energy.

In addition to providing a lightning evaluation of your defense chances, dummy's point count can tell you what *kind* of defense tactics may pay best. If dummy has overbid, then a tight-wad defense aimed at giving absolutely nothing away is indicated; but if dummy seems to be loaded, the odds could well favor daring—or even desperate—measures.

In making your first tentative assessment of the type of defense operation that may be needed, you should take account of one more factor: the position of your own cards in relation to the enemy high cards. If your high cards seem to be favorably placed, this in itself may be enough to capsize the contract, so you should be more inclined to play a conservative defense. Example:

NORTH	SOUTH
1♣	1◇
1♠	1NT
2NT	3NT
pass	

west holds: ♠ 5 4 3   ♡ K J 8 2   ◇ A J 8 3 2   ♣ 6

In some situations—for example, if you thought dummy held a long and solid suit that could provide enough tricks for game— you might be justified in launching a desperate attack on the diamond suit even though South has bid it. But this is not advisable here, since all the signs are that the cards lie extremely badly for South, whose strength is expected to be mainly in the red suits. West has these suits tightly held, and it is extremely probable that East has a half nelson on dummy's black suits. Therefore West should expect the contract to fail, and should play a passive defense that gives nothing away. The spade opening lead is most likely to achieve this objective.

Notice that this type of thumbnail appraisal is aimed principally at getting you in the right *mood* for winning defense: there is no easy substitute for the solid figuring that is needed before key plays can safely be made. But just as a poet is more likely to think beautiful thoughts on a sunset fishing trip than in a canning factory, so are you more likely to latch onto a bright defensive operation if your mind is already searching the correct sector of the wide range of defensive possibilities.

Point-Count Defense

Writers on defense play—usually men—tend to be perfectionists. They urge you to recapitulate the bidding in your mind, asking yourself the meaning of every bid. They remind you to figure out the declarer's hand pattern and his approximate point count before you make a vital play. And they emphasize that you should deduce information from every card that is played.

All this is very fine. It would also help if you had a slide rule, an ice pack, unlimited time and a couple of professors to give advice and counsel. Unfortunately, you don't have any of these things at a bridge table. And because you don't, the advice of ivory-tower teachers can be as much use to a practical woman as an etiquette manual in a rush-hour subway.

The truth is that although *some* defense decisions can be made after cool and deliberate calculation, others have to be made quickly—*too* quickly for you to sift all the evidence as carefully as you would like to. Take, for example, the decision whether or not to high-low, or "echo" as it is commonly called. (If you hesitate before echoing—or before *not* echoing—you may thereby give your partner unauthorized information and subject her to an ethical strain.) Or the decision whether to cover an enemy honor when it is led. (If you hesitate, you telegraph the position of your high card.) Or the decision whether you hop up with an ace when the declarer leads toward a king-jack combination. (If you hesitate, the declarer can no longer take a losing position.)

How to make accurate decisions fast can be the toughest of problems, and not even a world champion aspires to do better than keep the percentage of errors low. Most players would probably score better if they made their decisions faster, even if this entails some loss of accuracy; and the tougher the opposition the more true this is. Some experts can deduce more from a seemingly-unimportant hesitation than Sherlock Holmes could figure out from a faint whiff of Oriental perfume in the room where the naval treaty disappeared. The more frequently you hesitate, the more you tip off your hand. I am not sure that this is not a more serious problem for women defenders than for men; since women, with their well-known sensitivity to public opinion, are inclined to attach rather too much weight to the importance of avoiding bloopers. This slows them down.

The problem of how to play quickly without making too many mistakes is most acute in the play to the first trick or two. By the time the play reaches the middle game, one has usually had the chance to do some figuring, but in the first few tricks a fast decision may be forced upon you before you are properly prepared. I have devised a little routine that helps to slash the incidence of wrong decisions in these situations.

As soon as the bidding seems about to subside, figure out approximately how many high-card points the declarer ought to have for the bids he has made. Add this to your own points, and as soon as dummy is spread add in dummy's points as well. By subtracting this total from 40, you know almost exactly how many points partner holds. And, most important, you know it immediately dummy's cards hit the table. By following this technique, you can play the kind of lightning defense that was needed on the following deal:

```
                 ♠ 7
                 ♡ K 9 8 6
                 ◇ K 8 3
                 ♣ Q 10 9 7 2
  ♠ Q 10 8 3     ┌─────────────┐     ♠ A 9 6 5 2
  ♡ 10 2         │    NORTH     │     ♡ Q J 3
  ◇ Q J 10 6     │ WEST   EAST  │     ◇ 7 5 2
  ♣ 8 6 4        │    SOUTH     │     ♣ K J
                 └─────────────┘
                 ♠ K J 4
                 ♡ A 7 5 4
                 ◇ A 9 4
                 ♣ A 5 3
```

SOUTH	NORTH
1NT	2♣
2♡	4♡
pass	

Since South was playing a standard notrump, East added South's minimum holding of 16 high-card points to her own 11 points, and reached a total of 27. As soon as West opened the diamond queen, East added in three more points for the queen-jack sequence that West was known to hold—and when North put down an eight-point dummy East had already tagged 38 of the 40 points in the deck. Aside from the diamond suit, therefore, West could not possibly hold better than a queen (not two jacks since three had already been accounted for) —which had to be the spade queen, since the others were visible.

A brief glance at dummy enabled East to put this information to work. The defenders were obviously slated for one spade trick and one trump, and they could not hope to win more than one club trick because the ace was known to be in South's hand. To beat the contract, therefore, E-W had to corral a diamond trick. And although South was marked with the spade king— which could provide a parking place for dummy's losing diamond —the chance that West might hold the spade queen created the possibility that South might take a losing position in the spade suit.

So when South, having won the diamond opening, cashed the ace and king of trumps and led the spade singleton from the table, East did not rise with the ace but played smoothly low. Predictably, South took the losing position by playing the jack, and West, after winning the trick with the queen, immediately fired back a diamond. Now there was no way South could avoid losing a diamond trick—and his four-heart contract.

Notice that to have any chance of beating the hand East not only had to duck the spade ace—she had to duck without any hesitation. East was able to do this only because the fast countdown on her partner's points had told her that the duck was the only real chance.

Such point-count defense can and should continue all the way through the deal. After your defense operation, based on your first fleeting assessment of the layout of the cards, has gotten under way, you should gain a steadily more accurate picture of where the declarer's points are located. On a great many deals, a point-count defender can figure out all the unseen holdings before the midway point of the hand is reached (with practice, this call will become as routine as knowing how many trumps are out), and this can frequently promote a "magic" defense.

```
                    ♠ 7 5 3
                    ♡ Q 10 7 6 5
                    ◇ Q J
                    ♣ K Q 9
 ♠ K Q 10      ┌─────────────────┐    ♠ J 9 8 2
 ♡ K 2         │      NORTH       │    ♡ J 9 4
 ◇ A 10 8 3    │                  │    ◇ 7 5 2
 ♣ 10 8 6 4    │ WEST      EAST   │    ♣ 7 5 3
               │                  │
               │      SOUTH       │
               └─────────────────┘
                    ♠ A 6 4
                    ♡ A 8 3
                    ◇ K 9 6 4
                    ♣ A J 2
```

SOUTH	NORTH
1NT	2♣
2◇	3NT
pass	

When a declarer has responded negatively to a Stayman inquiry, it is inadvisable to open a sketchy minor suit, since declarer must have good cards in the minors. Therefore, West led the king of spades and East encouraged. South held off for two rounds but when South won the third spade lead and laid down the heart ace West realized it was not necessary to play quickly to avoid giving the declarer free information. West therefore took time out to figure a point-count defense.

South could not hold fewer than 16 points on his notrump opening; West could see 22 more points in her own hand and in dummy, so East could not hold more than two. One of East's points was known to be the spade jack, and it would not help the defenders' chances if the other was the club jack. West therefore decided that the three-notrump contract was unbeatable unless East held the heart jack.

Accordingly, West dropped the heart king under South's ace, thereby building East an entry card for the long spade. After West's spectacular unblocking play, there was nothing South could do to salvage the contract, since he could not win nine tricks without dummy's long hearts; and if he allowed East to gain the lead the defenders could cash a total of five tricks.

Help for Partner

When nearly all the defenders' points are located in the hand of one player—as in the last deal, where West held 12 of the defenders' 14 points—it is often easier for that player to figure out a cute defense than it would be if the points were more evenly distributed. This explains why plenty of defenders who keep right on their toes when they hold most of the key cards tend to relax and leave partner to carry the banner when they hold a poor hand. But women are less prone to this error than men, and their thrifty housekeeping instincts can help them eke out the best defense even when they hold a low-power hand. Suppose you are East in the following situation:

♠	J 7
♡	K 8 3 2
◇	J 9 4
♣	Q 9 4 3

NORTH	♠ Q 10 8 3
	♡ 6 4
EAST	◇ 8 6 3
	♣ 10 8 5 2

SOUTH	NORTH
1 ♡	2 ♡
4 ♡	pass

When West opens the spade ace a pessimistic East might think that defense prospects had nose-dived to oblivion, since West's lead has patently blown a trick by setting up South's unsupported king. But a more buoyant East will realize that her weak hand could well prove a hidden asset, because a declarer will usually assume that the defenders' high cards are more or less equally divided between two defending hands. South may therefore get a nasty shock when West turns up with a larger-than-expected share of missing cards. If E-W can avoid giving away any more free tricks the game may yet be saved. This is where East can come through for the team, by making sure she plays the correct card to the first trick. Can you select that card?

A woman, with her more practical outlook on life, is much more likely to come up with the right card in this situation. Instead of sitting and thinking bitter thoughts because West has blown a trick on the opening lead, East should brightly encourage a spade continuation by dropping the eightspot. West may be disappointed when she finds East hasn't got the king—but the spade continuation must be safe, and West would be a lot more disappointed if she were encouraged by a low spade from East to shift to another suit, since this could well cost another defensive trick.

If you are a devout believer in the admirable principle that one shouldn't mislead one's partner, you may dislike the idea of encouraging West's spade opening on the grounds that it may fool West into thinking you hold the king. Furthermore, you may argue that if West knew that *South* held the king, West might want to shift to another suit instead of continuing spades. Such reasoning would normally be sound, but in this particular instance we can be a hundred percent sure that West has no safe suit to lead, otherwise he would not have opened an unsupported ace.

The chance to play big defense on small hands is much more

common than might be supposed—and I have found that the male half of a mixed partnership is much more likely to miss chances through undue pessimism than is a woman. Consider the following type of bidding sequence:

NORTH	EAST	SOUTH	WEST
1 ♠	pass	1NT	pass
2NT	pass	3NT	pass
pass	pass		

west holds: ♠ 8 6   ♡ J 10 9 3   ♢ J 9 5 2   ♣ 7 6 4

A gloomy male will immediately decide that this is just another laydown game for the opponents and will merely spend the rest of the deal wondering whether the Dow Jones average is ever going to get back to what it was six months ago. A bright defender, on the other hand, will take notice of the lack of conviction in the N-S bidding sequence and will register a warm mental vote of thanks to East, who clearly holds somewhere around 13 points and who very astutely has kept out of the bidding. This means that South, who has limped into three notrump on a wing and a prayer, is going to have a hard time making his contract, since he will not expect the defenders' strength to be massed mainly in East's hand. So, provided West makes her normal opening lead—the heart jack—and thereafter keeps on her toes, the contract is probably headed for defeat. Notice that although it is quite likely East holds strength in spades, a spade opening might alert South to the possibility of bad breaks.

Although it is often the distaff side of a team that produces help for partner in these situations, I recall many occasions in my partnership with Charlie Goren when the roles were reversed. Charlie found a big play when he held the small East hand on the following deal.

```
                    ♠  A K J
                    ♡  10 9 4
                    ◇  10 7 5
                    ♣  A J 8 3
♠  7 3          ┌─────────────────┐      ♠  6 5 2
♡  A K 6        │     NORTH       │      ♡  J 8 7 2
◇  A J 8 6 3    │  WEST     EAST  │      ◇  9 4
♣  7 6 2        │     SOUTH       │      ♣  Q 10 5 4
                └─────────────────┘
                    ♠  Q 10 9 8 4
                    ♡  Q 5 3
                    ◇  K Q 2
                    ♣  K 9
```

SOUTH	WEST	NORTH	EAST
pass	1 ◇	pass	pass
2 ♠	pass	3 ♠	pass
4 ♠	pass	pass	pass

After a cautious first-round pass, South more than made up in the later rounds of bidding. His reopening bid of two spades was a reasonable effort, but when North could not raise all the way to game South should have been satisfied with a partial.

Although the four-spade contract was full of holes, South might well have brought it home after I, all unsuspecting, had led the heart king from the West hand. With the heart jack favorably located in East's hand, my heart opening meant that South would lose only two tricks in that suit, whereas had I found the safe trump lead South would have found it difficult to avoid three heart losers.

Charlie, sitting East, knew I had not found the lead of the century, but he wasted no time crying over spilt milk; instead he gave me a come-on with the eight. Charlie correctly figured that—with the heart king already out of the way—South could build a heart trick any time he wanted by leading dummy's ten and finessing against the jack, so he preferred to encourage a heart continuation rather than run the risk that I might shift dangerously to some other suit. I obediently continued hearts and, after South's queen had won the third round, South did his best to land the contract by playing three rounds of clubs, ruffing in his hand. When the club queen failed to drop, South cashed three rounds of trumps and led a small diamond to the king, hoping that I would flub the end game. This was the position:

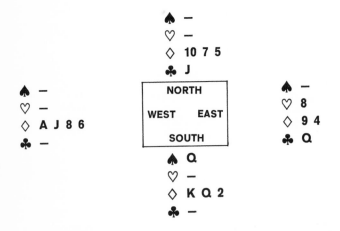

When South led a diamond from the table and put on the king, he hoped I'd win the ace—which would be a fatal blunder, since on my enforced diamond return dummy's tenspot would win the gamegoing trick. Fortunately, the deal was easy to read at this stage. It was now obvious that East had started with the club queen and heart jack, and he would not have passed my one-diamond opening if he had also held the diamond queen. So I let South's king win and waited to collect two diamond tricks.

Notice the value of East's thoughtful come-on at the first trick: had East discouraged the heart opening, I might have taken it into my head to shift to a club, in which case South could have maneuvered to build a gamegoing trick in that suit via a ruffing finesse against East.

On the next deal, the woman who played big defense on a small East hand was a ranking expert; but even if she hadn't been, she might still have come up with the winning move by following the now familiar principle that if a shift can't win, you should encourage partner to continue the suit he has opened.

```
                        ♠ 8 6 5
                        ♡ Q 2
                        ◇ A Q 10
                        ♣ A K Q J 9
  ♠ A 9 4           ┌─── NORTH ───┐      ♠ 10 3
  ♡ A K 9 7 6 4     │             │      ♡ 10 8 3
  ◇ 5 2             │ WEST    EAST│      ◇ 9 7 6 4
  ♣ 10 3            │             │      ♣ 7 6 5 4
                    └─── SOUTH ───┘
                        ♠ K Q J 7 2
                        ♡ J 5
                        ◇ K J 8 3
                        ♣ 8 2
```

NORTH	EAST	SOUTH	WEST
1 ♣	pass	1 ♠	2 ♡
3 ◇	pass	4 ◇	pass
4 ♠	pass	pass	pass

North hoped his three-diamond bid might prod South into three notrump if he held a heart guard, but when this failed N-S settled for the reasonable spade game. This seemed to depend only on a favorable trump break, but E-W found a way to amass four tricks even though the trump suit divided 3-2.

When West opened the heart king, East did not routinely drop her lowest heart, because she appreciated this might cause West to shift to a diamond, hoping East held the king; furthermore, East realized that after cashing the heart king and ace the defenders would have no chance of any further tricks in the plain suits, since dummy's hand was too strong. The setting trick could come only from the trump suit, so East started an echo by dropping the heart ten on the opening lead even though she realized this might cause West to present declarer with a ruff and discard. West duly cashed a second heart and continued with a third, which South ruffed on the table. When South next played a trump to the king, West won the ace and fired back a fourth heart, which East ruffed with the ten. South had to overruff with the jack, making West's nine good for the setting trick.

Another way you can play big defense on small hands is by the careful selection of discards when you show out of a suit. Imagination as well as empathy are needed to appreciate how East can help her partner in a situation like the following:

♠ K 10 9
♡ 9 5 2
◇ K Q 10 8
♣ 8 6 5

NORTH	♠ 6 2
	♡ J 10 8 7 6 3
EAST	◇ 7 5
	♣ 7 4 3

SOUTH	NORTH
3NT	4NT
6NT	pass

West leads the club king, South wins the ace and rattles off a long diamond suit. As East, what is your first discard?

Even though East holds only one point, she can play an important part in the defense by helping her partner, who is sure to be under pressure. At the first opportunity, East should drop the heart jack, telling West that East can look after the long cards in hearts. If West happens to hold the heart queen, the imaginative heart discard may be the only way to tell West that it is safe to ditch hearts in order to look after the other suits.

Help from the Opposition

There are not too many bridge situations where an innocent and trusting nature pays off, but one such situation, contrary to much that has been written, is in defense play. True, it is better to believe your partner than the opposition. But it is better to believe the opponents than to believe no one at all. Only if you have faith in the soundness of the opposition bidding are you likely to come up with the defense that East produced on this deal:

```
        ♠ Q J 2
        ♡ A
        ◇ 10 5 4
        ♣ K Q J 9 8 4
   ┌──────────────┐      ♠ A 6 4
   │ NORTH        │      ♡ Q 10 9 4 2
   │        EAST  │      ◇ K J 9 2
   │              │      ♣ 10
   └──────────────┘
```

NORTH	SOUTH
1♣	1♡
2♣	3NT
pass	

When West opens the spade ten and dummy plays the jack, how should East plan the play?

Because there is no reason to distrust South's three-notrump bid, East should immediately place him with a high card in each of the unbid suits in a hand counting at least 13 points. This means South must hold the spade king, so if East wins the ace and returns a spade South will easily make game via two spade tricks, two hearts and probably six clubs.

Furthermore, it is no use ducking the opening spade lead to see what happens; what is most likely to happen is that South will produce the club ace and rattle off his game contract. (South must surely hold the heart king for his one heart bid and that card will provide a ninth trick without South's having to touch spades again.)

If you trust your opponents, there is only one chance to beat the hand—a diamond shift. East should therefore go up with the spade ace on the opening lead and fire back the diamond *jack*—a backward finesse that is the only way to collect four fast diamond tricks if West holds ace-third. The full deal was:

```
                    ♠ Q J 2
                    ♡ A
                    ◇ 10 5 4
                    ♣ K Q J 9 5 4
  ♠ 10 9 8 5 3    ┌──────────────┐    ♠ A 6 4
  ♡ 8 6           │    NORTH     │    ♡ Q 10 9 4 2
  ◇ A 8 3         │ WEST   EAST  │    ◇ K J 9 2
  ♣ 8 7 3         │    SOUTH     │    ♣ 10
                  └──────────────┘
                    ♠ K 7
                    ♡ K J 7 5 3
                    ◇ Q 7 6
                    ♣ A 6 2
```

On East's shift to the diamond jack, South was helpless; whether he covered or not the defenders were able to run four diamond tricks.

Even more profitable than trusting your opponents' bidding is trusting their card play. People sometimes make bids they know to be wrong but they very, very seldom make *plays* which they know to be wrong. Because it is normally safe to trust a competent declarer's card play, East should have no trouble finding a safe discard in a situation like the following:

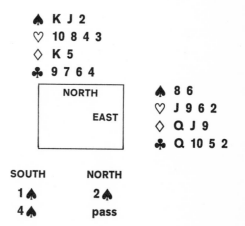

♠ K J 2
♡ 10 8 4 3
◇ K 5
♣ 9 7 6 4

NORTH

EAST

♠ 8 6
♡ J 9 6 2
◇ Q J 9
♣ Q 10 5 2

SOUTH	NORTH
1 ♠	2 ♠
4 ♠	pass

West leads a small trump and South immediately pulls three more rounds, while West follows suit. If East discards wrongly on the third round of spades, she is very likely to give away a trick, but fortunately East can ditch a diamond with no fear. If South held more than two diamonds he would surely have ruffed one before pulling trumps.

The more you can trust the declarer to play his cards correctly, the easier it is to come up with the winning answer on a problem deal like this one:

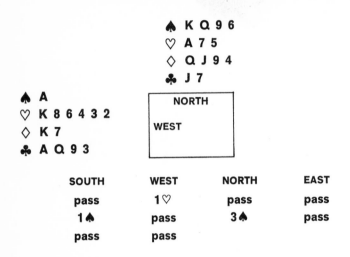

	♠ K Q 9 6		
	♡ A 7 5		
	♢ Q J 9 4		
	♣ J 7		

♠ A
♡ K 8 6 4 3 2
♢ K 7
♣ A Q 9 3

NORTH

WEST

SOUTH	WEST	NORTH	EAST
pass	1♡	pass	pass
1♠	pass	3♠	pass
pass	pass		

Sitting West, you elect to open the heart four and dummy's ace wins, East dropping the nine and South the ten. The king of trumps is led and, having won the ace, you have to be careful to find the right return. Which card do you play from the West hand?

Although South is marked with most of the missing cards, West must hope to add two clubs and a diamond to the trump trick she has already won. However, it may be important to grab those club tricks before South can drive out the diamond king, since thereafter discards will be available on dummy's long diamonds.

Fortunately, South is known to be a competent card player and he can be trusted to have made the correct play on the opening heart lead. Had South held the heart queen he would have let the heart opening ride around to the closed hand, so it is a cinch East holds that card. Having won the trump ace, West therefore underleads the heart king, allowing East to win the queen, and return a club.

The complete layout:

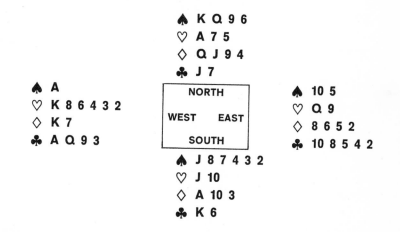

Notice that if West cashes the heart king instead of under-leading it, South drives out the diamond king and ditches a club on dummy's long diamonds.

The extent to which you should trust your opponents is something that everyone has to figure out for herself. You have to be a psychologist, and you have to have a shrewd idea of how capable your opponents are. Granted these two essentials, there is every prospect that you can outguess the declarer on many deals.

Thus, when a capable declarer has two different lines of play that he can follow, he will rightly defer the choice as long as possible. When defending against such a player, one should be suspicious of any seemingly crucial play that he makes very early in the game, because the chances are that it is not a crucial play at all, but merely something designed to give him an extra chance while keeping all his main chances hidden until later. Complicated shell-game reasoning of this kind is what underlies the brilliant defense coups that experts sometimes produce:

```
                    ♠ 8 6 5
                    ♡ A Q 10 7
                    ◇ A Q J 9
                    ♣ Q 2
  ♠ A 4 2          ┌─────────────┐        ♠ J 10 7 3
  ♡ 9 8 6          │    NORTH     │        ♡ 5 3 2
  ◇ K 8 5 2        │ WEST    EAST │        ◇ 10 6 4
  ♣ 7 5 3          │    SOUTH     │        ♣ 9 6 4
                   └─────────────┘
                    ♠ K Q 9
                    ♡ K J 4
                    ◇ 7 3
                    ♣ A K J 10 8
```

SOUTH	NORTH
1♣	1◇
2NT	6NT
pass	

On the lead of the heart nine, South won in dummy and, after consideration, played a spade to the king. West knew it was extremely unlikely South would lead toward an unsupported spade king at such an early stage of the play, since he clearly held other, and less dangerous, chances of building the tricks he needed for slam: for example, by tackling the diamond suit. South's play in the spade suit, therefore, was not a neck-or-nothing play that staked everything on finding the ace well-placed, but was merely designed to spy out the lie of the land. West therefore unhesitatingly let the king win. After cashing a few winners, South re-entered dummy and led another spade, expecting to gather a slam-going trick with the queen and so avoid risking the diamond finesse; but this time West won the ace and returned

a spade to her partner's jack. Had West released the spade ace
the first time, South would have been compelled to take the winning diamond finesse for his twelfth trick.

On the next deal, the inference that East drew would have
been proper against almost any declarer—though East had to show
high imagination to make use of it.

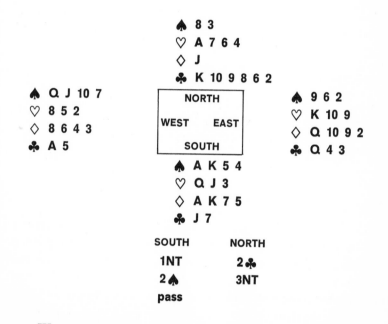

```
                    ♠ 8 3
                    ♡ A 7 6 4
                    ◇ J
                    ♣ K 10 9 8 6 2
♠ Q J 10 7        ┌─────────────┐        ♠ 9 6 2
♡ 8 5 2          │    NORTH    │        ♡ K 10 9
◇ 8 6 4 3        │ WEST   EAST │        ◇ Q 10 9 2
♣ A 5            │    SOUTH    │        ♣ Q 4 3
                  └─────────────┘
                    ♠ A K 5 4
                    ♡ Q J 3
                    ◇ A K 7 5
                    ♣ J 7
```

SOUTH	NORTH
1NT	2♣
2♠	3NT
pass	

West opened the spade queen. South won the trick with the
ace and led the club jack, finessed to East's queen. By this time,
East had a tremendous amount of information available about
South's hand.

Had South held the ace of clubs, he would surely have cashed
that card before leading the jack. He couldn't have a singleton
club and open with one notrump. Hence, he had started with jack
and one. He had shown four spades in response to Stayman, and

his winning the trick with the ace did not conceal the king, with which he was marked by West's opening lead of the queen. Returning a spade would set up two tricks for the defense, and the defenders would also get West's ace of clubs, but that would be all. If North-South had been playing 15–18-point notrumps, it might be possible for West to be holding the king of diamonds. But South's minimum was 16 points, so he had to hold both the diamond ace and king and a shift to that suit was hopeless. But, since South was known to hold only two clubs, he would have to hold onto North's ace of hearts as a re-entry to the club suit.

Instead of blindly returning spades, East shifted to the king of hearts! South could not afford to spend dummy's ace without cutting himself off from the long clubs. When he ducked the trick, East shifted back to spades to sink the contract.

East's defense was, in part, based on being able to rely on South's failure to cash the club ace as a certain indication that he did not hold that card.

Be Ready to Take Over

One of the minor hazards a woman has to combat when she plays bridge with a man is that her thinking tends to be geared to the theory of The Dominant Male. In everyday life we may be right to respect this quaint old notion and to take the trouble to employ sufficient subtlety to seem guiltless of back-seat driving. But there are many defense situations where such refinement can be costly. Quite often you do not merely have to brave the charge of back-seat driving—you have to lean over and grab the steering wheel with both hands.

On this deal in a mixed-team championship, East was playing with a world-famous male expert and her error was induced by her modest reluctance to take command of the defense.

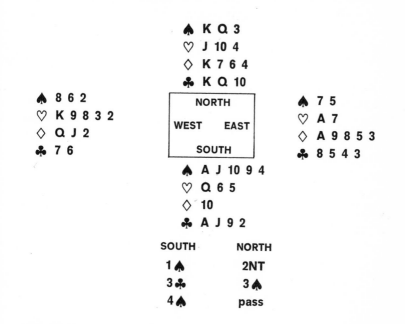

♠ K Q 3
♡ J 10 4
◇ K 7 6 4
♣ K Q 10

♠ 8 6 2
♡ K 9 8 3 2
◇ Q J 2
♣ 7 6

NORTH
WEST   EAST
SOUTH

♠ 7 5
♡ A 7
◇ A 9 8 5 3
♣ 8 5 4 3

♠ A J 10 9 4
♡ Q 6 5
◇ 10
♣ A J 9 2

SOUTH	NORTH
1♠	2NT
3♣	3♠
4♠	pass

West opened a low heart and, having won the ace, East fired back the seven spot, all bright-eyed and bushy-tailed and awaiting a heart ruff. East expected that the diamond ace would then supply the setting trick.

But the defense lost its way. On the second round of hearts, South blandly dropped the queen—and when he won the king West took the eminently reasonable position that South might have no more hearts, in which case it would be essential to shift to a diamond. West therefore returned the diamond queen. East headed dummy's king with the ace but South claimed the rest of the tricks.

Although it was West who failed to give his partner a heart ruff, he was not to blame. East could have made sure of beating the contract had she taken charge of the defense by playing off the diamond ace before returning the heart seven. Cashing the diamond ace would have made it plain to West that there were no more tricks to be garnered from that suit.

Furthermore, if on a different layout the diamond ace gets ruffed, East has the consolation that the contract was probably unbeatable. But South is very unlikely to be void of diamonds since this would place West with ◇ Q J 10 2, and he would probably have opened the queen. East was quite capable of figuring this out—but a psychological aversion to taking over the captaincy kept her from the winning path. Such inhibitions have to be conquered when you play bridge with a man.

Similar to being too shy to take charge are the dangers of following card-play conventions too rigidly. In a social sense women are both the originators and the upholders of convention, and this makes them prone to stick *too* closely to card-play rules. Would you have been unconventional enough on this deal?

	♠ K J 10 8	
	♡ K Q 3	
	◇ A 5 3	
	♣ 8 6 5	

♠ 7 6 5 3	NORTH	♠ A Q 4
♡ 6 4		♡ 8 5 2
◇ Q 10 6	WEST EAST	◇ K 9 8 2
♣ 10 7 4 2	SOUTH	♣ K J 9

	♠ 9 2	
	♡ A J 10 9 7	
	◇ J 7 4	
	♣ A Q 3	

SOUTH	NORTH
1 ♡	1 ♠
2 ♡	4 ♡
pass	

West opened the club deuce and a fast countdown told East that her partner could not be expected to contribute more than about two points to the defense. If West held the club queen the contract could probably be defeated via two club tricks and two spades, but if West held the diamond queen instead, there would not be enough tricks to be garnered in the club suit and it would be important to shift to diamonds as soon as possible. East therefore had to find out which queen West held. East's method of doing so was slightly unconventional. But it was certainly a very effective means.

On the club opening lead, East did not automatically put up the king; instead, she played the jack, deliberately finessing against her partner. It was a safe play, since by totaling the points, she knew South must hold the club ace. If South also held the queen, which indeed she did, neither East's jack nor her king would be good. When South won the club queen, East knew that the only hope was to find West with the diamond queen, so after South had taken the losing spade finesse East fired back a diamond. When she regained the lead with the spade ace, East was able to cash two diamond tricks, thereby wrecking the contract. Of course, if East's play of the club jack had fetched the ace from South, East would have known that there were two club tricks to be obtained.

If East conventionally plays the club king on the opening lead, she does not know which suit to play when she gets in with the spade queen—and if she mistakenly elects to play a club the defense cannot possibly win more than the ten of clubs and the ace and queen of spades.

There are probably more exceptions to the "third hand high" convention than most defenders realize. It is sometimes possible that you can safely pull a play like the one East made on the preceding deal when there is a danger that the declarer may win an unnecessary trick.

```
                    ♠ A Q 10 8 3
                    ♡ 9 2
                    ◇ J 10 7 4
                    ♣ K 7
♠ 7 5                                   ♠ K 6 4 2
♡ Q 8 6 4 3         NORTH               ♡ A J 5
◇ 9 6 5        WEST        EAST         ◇ A 3 2
♣ 10 8 5            SOUTH               ♣ 6 4 2
                    ♠ J 9
                    ♡ K 10 7
                    ◇ K Q 8
                    ♣ A Q J 9 3
```

SOUTH	NORTH
1NT	2♣
2◇	3♠
3NT	

When the opponents employ a Stayman-type sequence in search of a major-suit contract, the defenders usually have plenty of information to work on. And on this deal the fact that East holds most of her team's high cards makes it easier for her to take control of defense tactics. Therefore when West leads the heart four, East should finesse the jack. East knows—partly from South's negative response to the Stayman inquiry and partly from West's lead of the four spot—that West holds exactly five hearts, but it is unlikely that he has an entry card. If East plays the heart ace on the opening lead South will automatically make game by holding up the king till the third round and driving out East's two aces at leisure.

By finessing the heart jack on the opening lead East virtually compels South to win the king immediately, since South cannot be sure that West does not hold the ace. And even if, on a different layout, East's unconventional maneuver allowed South to win the heart queen, this would not be a serious matter, since South would not be able to run off enough tricks for game.

Women are sometimes too loyal to convention when they have to lead from an honor combination such as K x x x. The fourth-best card is of course the normal lead; but if you follow the rules too closely your partner may get wrong ideas in a situation like the following:

♠ K 9 6
♡ A 3
◇ 7 6 5
♣ A Q J 3 2

	NORTH		♠ A Q J 2
			♡ K 6
	EAST		◇ K 9 4 3
			♣ 9 6 4

NORTH	SOUTH
1♣	1♡
2♣	3♡
4♡	pass

West opens a small spade, dummy plays low and to East's dismay South ruffs away the jack. When South leads the trump queen and lets it ride around to the king, East quickly realizes that the defenders have got to win three fast diamond tricks to beat the contract, so she fires back a diamond. But *which* diamond?

If East plays back a small card South may well make his contract even if West holds ◇ A J x—because, having won the jack, West may well take it into his head that East holds the club king and not the diamond king. If West does indeed come to this conclusion, he will exit passively after he has won the diamond jack, waiting for East to regain the lead and play another diamond. South will now make his contract—and it will be partly East's fault, because when East wins her trump trick, she should slap down the diamond *king,* saving West a headache.

The trouble with these unconventional plays is that if they are successful they may tempt you to go even further and engage in an activity that used to be considered downright shocking: false-carding. Although the habitual false-carder is no longer the social outcast that he was considered in whist-playing days, I earnestly advise against employing such maneuvers when there is any chance that they can mislead your partner. However, I do advise keeping an eye open for the opportunities that sometimes come along to play false cards that may mislead the declarer *but cannot mislead partner.* Following is a fine example of this subtle and little-known art.

	♠ K 9 8	
	♡ Q 10 6	
	◇ 10 6 5	
	♣ A J 10 2	

♠ 4 2		♠ A Q
♡ 9 5 3	**NORTH**	♡ 8 7 4 2
◇ A J 4 3 2	**WEST EAST**	◇ K Q 9 8
♣ Q 9 8	**SOUTH**	♣ 6 4 3

	♠ J 10 7 6 5 3	
	♡ A K J	
	◇ 7	
	♣ K 7 5	

NORTH	SOUTH
pass	1 ♠
2 ♣	2 ♠
3 ♠	4 ♠
pass	

West cashed the diamond ace and continued with a small diamond, but on the second round East did not make the normal play of the queen because she realized that this would tip off the fact that she held the king as well. Realizing that it might be important to conceal the location of the defenders' points, East false-carded by playing the king. This did not, of course, deceive West one little bit, because West knew the true position immediately when South ruffed. (Furthermore, had South, on a different layout, followed suit to the second diamond lead, West would not have been aggrieved at the deception, because East's two solid gold trump tricks would mean the automatic defeat of the contract.)

But East's false card with the diamond king *did* fool South. After clearing trumps, South eventually had to take a position on the location of the club queen. And with no real clues to guide him, South happened to take the losing position. Had East routinely played the diamond queen on the second round of the suit, thereby telegraphing the location of the king as well, South would eventually have been able to place East with a total of 11 points in spades and diamonds. Since East had failed to open the bidding, South would have reasoned that East could not hold the club queen as well.

Quizzes

QUIZ 1   Which card should West lead in each of the following situations? Your answer should depend on whether the bidding suggests that *active* or *passive* defense is advisable.

west holds:		the bidding:			
		WEST	NORTH	EAST	SOUTH
1	♠ J 10 5		1♣	pass	1♠
	♡ K 3	pass	1♣	pass	1♠
	◇ 9 7 6 5 2	pass	3♠	pass	4◇
	♣ Q 4 3	pass	4♠	pass	pass
2	♠ J 10 7 3	WEST	NORTH	EAST	SOUTH
	♡ 10 8 2	pass	1♣	pass	1♡
	◇ A Q 9 3	pass	1♠	pass	1 NT
	♣ 6 4	pass	2♡	pass	3♡
		pass	4♡	pass	pass
3	♠ 6 5 4	WEST	NORTH	EAST	SOUTH
	♡ K J 9	pass	pass	pass	1◇
	◇ A J 8	pass	1♠	pass	2♣
	♣ Q 9 4 3	pass	2◇	pass	2 NT
		pass	3 NT	pass	pass
4	♠ 7 6 4	WEST	NORTH	EAST	SOUTH
	♡ 9 4 3	pass	1◇	pass	1♠
	◇ A 6	pass	3◇	pass	3 NT
	♣ A Q 10 9 2	pass	pass	pass	
5	♠ 9 2	WEST	NORTH	EAST	SOUTH
	♡ 8 7	pass	1◇	double	1 NT
	◇ Q J 10 2	pass	2 NT	pass	3 NT
	♣ Q 9 5 3 2	double	pass	pass	pass

Answers

1 *Heart king.* Active defense is the order of the day, since N-S have bid very strongly and there is no indication that the cards lie in any way badly for the declarer. The best chance to sink the contract seems to be via a heart ruff, though partner will still have to produce another trick from somewhere or other.

2 *Heart two.* A trump lead is frequently the most passive move you can make—and since N-S have limped unconvincingly into the four-heart contract there is every chance that it will fail provided West gives nothing away with her opening lead. Furthermore, South's one-notrump bid suggests that he holds something in diamonds. Since West holds command of that suit it may be wise to slash dummy's ruffing potential as much as possible.

3 *Spade six.* Again the E-W bidding sequence is unimpressive and West can reasonably hope that the contract is headed for defeat on passive defense. Since South has bid diamonds, clubs and notrumps, the chances are he is short in spades, so a spade opening should be safe and may well find East at home in the suit. Incidentally, when you have no safe honor sequence to lead from—such as Q J 10—a lead from a sequence of small cards such as 6 5 4 is usually best, since such a lead is very unlikely to give a trick away.

4 *Club ace.* On N-S's confident bidding it seems the declarer will have plenty of potential tricks if he is given time to develop them, but it is highly improbable that he can scamper away with the game contract without first developing dummy's long diamond suit. Therefore West can well afford to risk establishing a club trick for South by making an active opening lead, provided she ensures establishing four winners in the suit. The advantage of leading the ace is that West can continue with the queen if dummy happens to show up with jack-doubleton; while if dummy's original holding proves to be king-doubleton, West can of course continue with a small card.

5 *Heart eight.* Since East has doubled for takeout and West holds five points in her own hand, N-S cannot possess the 26 high-card points that are normally needed for game in notrump. Furthermore, West can calculate that the hand is likely to play extremely badly for the declarer: East is certain to be strong in the major suits, while West has both minors sewn up—though her holdings are not quite strong enough to make a lead of either minor suit completely safe. Since the contract seems certain to fail on passive defense, West should content herself with giving nothing away on the opening lead.

Notice that, in the interests of safety, the club opening is best avoided, since South, who failed to bid a major or support diamonds, may hold strength in that suit.

QUIZ 2   N-S are playing the standard 16–18-point notrump, plus the Stayman convention. When West leads the diamond king, which card should East play?

♠ Q 10 8 3
♡ K Q 10 5 4
♢ Q 5
♣ 9 6

	NORTH		♠ J 9 2
			♡ J 8 7
		EAST	♢ 9 6 2
			♣ Q J 10 4

the bidding:

WEST	NORTH	EAST	SOUTH
pass	pass	pass	1 NT
pass	2 ♣	pass	2 ♠
pass	4 ♠	pass	pass
pass			

Answer

The diamond six. West's lead of the diamond king indicates that he also holds the ace, and a point-count calculation suggests that even if South holds a minimum one-notrump opening West cannot contribute more than another king to the defense. If this is the club king, South cannot be stopped from making his contract, since he will lose just two diamonds and one club. But if West holds the *trump* king, he may be able to hand East a fourth-round diamond ruff. West must therefore be encouraged to continue diamonds and although the declarer will win the third round of the suit East will get a killing ruff when West regains the lead with the king of trumps.

QUIZ *3*   West opens the club nine and dummy plays the ace, continuing with a trump to South's queen, which wins. South now leads a small trump and West plays the king. What should East discard?

```
          ♠ A 9 3
          ♡ J 8
          ◇ J 8 6
          ♣ A K Q 10 2
     ┌──────────────┐   ♠ 10 8 7
     │    NORTH      │   ♡ Q 10 9 5 3 2
     │         EAST  │   ◇ 3
     │              │   ♣ J 6 4
     └──────────────┘
```

the bidding:

WEST	NORTH	EAST	SOUTH
1 ♠	2 ♣	pass	2 ◇
pass	4 ◇	pass	5 ◇
pass	pass	pass	

Answer

The heart ten. It is pretty obvious that West started life with ◇ A K x, and has held off one round to give East a chance to make an informative discard. East must select this discard with great care, since West evidently needs help in finding the correct return.

East's normal discard would be a small spade, since her spades are weaker than her hearts, but unfortunately she does not possess a spade small enough to make this message clear. There is a danger that if East pitches the spade seven West may interpret this as a come-on, so it will be much more helpful to discard an encouraging heart, even though East's highest heart is only the queen.

Notice that West would surely have led a spade initially if he held both king and queen, so the only real chance to beat the contract is to set up a heart trick before South can pull trumps and pitch her heart losers on dummy's clubs. The full deal would well be:

	♠ A 9 3	
	♡ J 8	
	◇ J 8 6	
	♣ A K Q 10 2	

♠ K J 6 5 2	NORTH	♠ 10 8 7
♡ K 7 4		♡ Q 10 9 5 3 2
◇ A K 2	WEST EAST	◇ 3
♣ 9 8	SOUTH	♣ J 6 4

	♠ Q 4	
	♡ A 6	
	◇ Q 10 9 7 5 4	
	♣ 7 5 3	

QUIZ 4   West opens the heart four, East plays the queen and South wins the king, immediately returning a small spade. How should West plan to beat the contract?

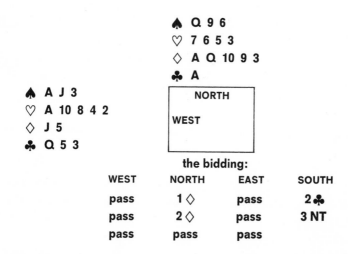

      ♠ Q 9 6
      ♡ 7 6 5 3
      ◇ A Q 10 9 3
      ♣ A

♠ A J 3
♡ A 10 8 4 2
◇ J 5
♣ Q 5 3

NORTH

WEST

the bidding:

WEST	NORTH	EAST	SOUTH
pass	1 ◇	pass	2 ♣
pass	2 ◇	pass	3 NT
pass	pass	pass	

Answer

Win the spade ace and lay down the heart ace. West should ask herself why the declarer has not tackled dummy's fine diamond suit, nor his own club suit, and why he is instead tackling a spindly spade holding. The answer must surely be that South holds the diamond king and club king, and is merely trying to snatch one trick in spades before running for home. West should therefore go right up with the spade ace and continue with the heart ace, since there is an excellent chance this will drop South's jack. And if South holds a second heart stop, it is unlikely West could have beaten the contract any other way, but the full deal is probably something like this:

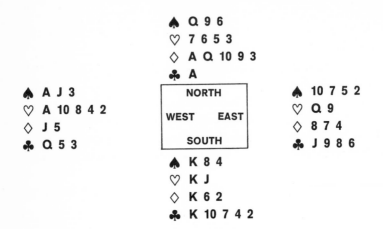

```
            ♠ Q 9 6
            ♡ 7 6 5 3
            ◇ A Q 10 9 3
            ♣ A
```

```
♠ A J 3                                   ♠ 10 7 5 2
♡ A 10 8 4 2      NORTH                   ♡ Q 9
◇ J 5          WEST    EAST               ◇ 8 7 4
♣ Q 5 3                                   ♣ J 9 8 6
                  SOUTH
```

```
            ♠ K 8 4
            ♡ K J
            ◇ K 6 2
            ♣ K 10 7 4 2
```

QUIZ 5   Be ready to take charge. West opens the spade four.
How should East plan to beat the contract?

```
            ♠ K Q 10 3
            ♡ J 8 5
            ◇ J 9 2
            ♣ A 6 4
```

```
              NORTH          ♠ A 9 7 5 2
                    EAST     ♡ A 6 3
                             ◇ Q
                             ♣ 10 8 3 2
```

the bidding:

WEST	NORTH	EAST	SOUTH
pass	pass	pass	1 ♡
pass	1 ♠	pass	2 ◇
pass	3 ♡	pass	3 ♠
pass	4 ♡	pass	pass
pass			

Answer

Win the spade ace and return the diamond queen. South's three-spade bid marks him with three cards in that suit, so West is obviously looking for an immediate ruff. But it so happens that East is able to figure a little farther ahead than West, so it is her duty to take charge of the defense. If East hands West an immediate ruff, the contract will probably be made, since West is unlikely to hold enough trumps for a second ruff when East regains the lead with the trump ace. South therefore will win the remainder of the tricks.

To prevent this, East must prepare the ground for a diamond ruff in her own hand before gratifying West's desire to ruff a spade. When East wins the trump ace, she returns a spade and, having ruffed, West will give East a killing diamond ruff. The full deal could be as follows:

```
                        ♠ K Q 10 3
                        ♡ J 8 5
                        ◇ J 9 2
                        ♣ A 6 4
   ♠ 4               ┌──────────────┐        ♠ A 9 7 5 2
   ♡ 7 4             │    NORTH      │        ♡ A 6 3
   ◇ 8 7 5 4 3       │ WEST    EAST  │        ◇ Q
   ♣ K Q 9 7 5       │    SOUTH      │        ♣ 10 8 3 2
                     └──────────────┘
                        ♠ J 8 6
                        ♡ K Q 10 9 2
                        ◇ A K 10 6
                        ♣ J
```

Bidding Valuation at a Glance

POINT COUNT

High-card points

ACE = 4 points

KING = 3 points

QUEEN = 2 points

JACK = 1 point

DEDUCT:

for singleton K, Q or J........1 point

for doubleton Q or J........1 point

for opener's aceless hand........1 point

ADD:

for four aces in hand........1 point

(Opener's hand)   *(Responder's hand in support of partner's suit)*

1........ DOUBLETON 1

2........ SINGLETON 2

3................ VOID 3

Distributional points may be added to high-card points to obtain total valuation. The different values assigned to singleton and void in the supporting hand in fact reflect a different form of trick-taking. In the responding hand, tricks are won by ruffing short suits; in opener's hand, tricks are most often won by suit LENGTH. But in most hands, there is little difference between short-suit and long-suit count, so single count of short suits in all cases is used for greater convenience.

An earlier method of valuation, originated by Ely Culbertson, was:

HONOR TRICKS

2 honor tricks = A-K of same suit

1½ honor tricks = A-Q of same suit
= K-Q-J of same suit

1 honor trick = A
= K-Q of same suit
= K-J-10 of same suit

½ honor trick = K-x of same suit
= Q-J-x of same suit

+ value = any Q, but not singleton

abt. ¼ hon. trick = any J combined with another

honor (but no singleton or doubleton and not A-K-Q-J)

abt. ¼ hon. trick = any singleton or void, but do not count more than one

QUICK TRICKS

—that is, defensive tricks when defending against an enemy contract:

A-K of same suit = 2

A-Q of same suit = 1½

A or K-Q of same suit = 1

K-x of same suit = ½

Conventions

The following is an explanation of the two Conventions (Blackwood and Stayman) mentioned in the text. Also included is a discussion of the Gerber Convention.

Blackwood Convention
The use of a four-notrump bid conventionally to discover the number of aces held by partner.

The conventional responses to the four-notrump bid are:
five clubs. . . . no ace or four aces
five diamonds. . . . one ace
five hearts. . . . two aces
five spades. . . . three aces

If the four-notrump bidder continues by bidding five notrump he is asking for kings in similar fashion. The five-notrump bid guarantees that the partnership holds all four aces.

In some circumstances it may be possible to play in five no-trump. If the Blackwood bidder bids an unbid suit at the five-level on the following round, he is requesting responder to bid five notrump.

Void Suits Void suits may not be counted as aces, but there are three methods in which voids can be indicated.

(a) Make the normal response, but at the level of six, to show the indicated number of aces and an unspecified void. Thus six clubs shows no ace and a void; six diamonds shows one ace and a void, etc. (Blackwood's recommendation).

(b) Bid six clubs to show one ace and a void; six diamonds to show two aces and a void.

(c) Bid five notrump to show two aces and a void; six of a

suit ranking below the agreed trump suit to show a void in that suit and one ace; six of the agreed trump suit to show one ace and a higher-ranking void.

Interference Bidding   The responder may still show the number of aces he holds after an opponent has intervened over four notrump thus: A one-step response (e.g. five spades over five hearts) would show one ace; a two-step response, two aces; and so on. A double would be natural, showing a desire to take a penalty, and a pass would usually show no ace. (But it might be made with a hand which could not afford to make the ace-showing response because of the level.)

Alternatively, a double can be used to show one ace, a one-step response to show two aces, and so on.

Four Notrump Non-conventional   There are a number of situations in which four notrump should be treated as a natural bid. This is so whenever the partnership has not bid a suit genuinely. For example:

SOUTH	NORTH	SOUTH	NORTH	SOUTH	NORTH
1NT	4NT	2♣*	2◇	1NT	2♣*
		2NT	4NT	2◇	4NT

using an artificial two-club bid

If during the auction one player bids three notrump and his partner bids four of a minor suit as a slam suggestion, a subsequent four-notrump bid by either player should be a natural sign-off bid. For example:

SOUTH	NORTH		SOUTH	NORTH
1♠	2♡		1♠	2♣
3 NT	4◇		3 NT	4♣
4 NT			4 NT	

In these sequences the final bid rejects the slam invitation and expresses a desire to play in four notrump.

Some play that four notrump is natural when no suit has been agreed, either directly or by inference. This covers a wide range.

For example:

SOUTH	NORTH
1 ♠	2 ♡
3 NT	4NT

Many players would regard this as conventional, but on the foregoing rule it would be natural.

SOUTH	NORTH
1 ♡	2 NT
4NT	

A direct raise from two notrump to four notrump at any stage can be regarded as natural. But judgment may be required when three notrump is followed by four notrump.

SOUTH	NORTH
1 ♠	3 ♡
3 NT	4 NT

This is conventional. North may be planning to play in either major but has had no opportunity to fix a suit below game.

Also, any sudden jump from a suit bid to four notrump is conventional.

Gerber Convention

A four-club bid asks partner how many aces he holds.

The responses are:
four diamonds.... no ace
four hearts.... one ace
four spades.... two aces
four notrump.... three aces
five clubs.... four aces
(Some play that four diamonds can be used instead of
five clubs to show the rare holding of four aces.)

The four-club bidder uses the next available bid to ask for kings on the same principle, but cannot use the agreed trump suit for this purpose. For example, four spades asks for kings over a response of four hearts, unless spades is the agreed trump suit, in which case four notrump then becomes the king-asking bid.

There may be difficulty in distinguishing a conventional four-club bid from a natural one. Some players restrict the use of the convention to situations in which no suit has been genuinely bid (e.g. after a 1 NT or 2 NT opening, or a conventional two-club bid followed by 2 NT or 3 NT).

If four clubs is used instead of Blackwood, there are three possible rules:

(a) Four clubs is conventional unless it is a direct club raise.

(b) Four clubs is conventional unless clubs have been genuinely bid by the partnership.

(c) Four clubs is conventional if it is a jump bid, or if a suit has been specifically agreed.

Stayman Convention

Two clubs in response to one notrump requires the opener to bid a major if he has one and otherwise to bid two diamonds. Stayman prefers a rebid of two spades holding both majors, but this is a detail of partnership style.

A subsequent rebid of two spades or two hearts by responder may be forcing for one round ("forcing Stayman") or not, at partnership choice.

A rebid of three clubs by responder is a sign-off, showing at least a six-card club suit and no interest in game.

After an opening bid of two notrump, three clubs asks for a major suit and three diamonds is a negative response. If the responder bids a major suit over three diamonds he promises a five-card suit.

Stayman After Overcall

When one notrump is overcalled, all minimum minor-suit bids by responder can be used to explore for major-suit contracts. After a two-club overcall, two diamonds asks for a major. Three clubs over a two-diamond overcall is similar; however, the bidding can stop at four of a minor suit. After a major-suit overcall, responder bids his long minor and promises length in the unbid major.

Questions of Bridge Law

How much do you know about the rules of bridge? Here are some questions to test your knowledge, followed by a concise version of the pertaining Laws of Contract Bridge.

What do You Know About an Insufficient Bid?

TRUE FALSE

1   If your bid is insufficient, you must make it sufficient with a higher bid.

2   An insufficient bid may be corrected by substituting a double.

3   You cannot ever correct an insufficient bid without your side being subject to a penalty.

4   You may be compelled to bid eight if there is no other way to correct your insufficient bid.

5   The auction has been:

WEST	NORTH	EAST	SOUTH
1 ♠	pass	1 ◇	1 ♡

North calls attention to East's insufficient bid, so East must make his bid sufficient.

Answers

1   FALSE. You may pass, if you accept the penalty.

2   FALSE. If the offender attempts to make his bid sufficient by a double or redouble, he is compelled instead to pass, and is subject to a penalty.

3   FALSE. If you make the bid sufficient with the minimum bid in the same declaration, there is no penalty.

4   FALSE. You may never be compelled to bid eight; in fact, a

bid of eight is illegal and must be cancelled, subject to penalties.
5   FALSE. South's one-heart bid has condoned the offense.

What do You Know About a Lead Out of Turn?

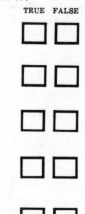

TRUE FALSE

1   If you lead a card before the auction is
concluded, your partner is barred for
one round of bidding.
2   If declarer leads from the wrong hand,
he may correct the error without penalty.
3   If a defender makes an opening lead out of
turn, his partner may be barred from leading
the suit for as long as he holds the lead.
4   If declarer leads when it is defender's turn,
declarer's card is exposed and must be played
at earliest opportunity.
5   If the wrong player leads and declarer
requires his partner to lead another suit, the
incorrect lead may be picked up and restored
to the offender's hand.

Answers
1   TRUE. And there may be further penalties if opponents become declarer.
2   FALSE. Declarer must lead the same suit from the correct
hand.
3   TRUE. If defender is barred from leading a suit, the prohi-
bition extends to subsequent leads, for as long as he holds the lead.
4   FALSE. Declarer is never subject to an exposed card penalty,
for the logical reason that information given cannot assist his
partner.
5   TRUE. Calling another penalty relieves the offender of the
exposed card penalty.

What Do You Know About the Revoke?

TRUE FALSE

1 The minimum penalty for an established
revoke is one trick.

☐ ☐

2 The dummy cannot revoke.

☐ ☐

3 There is no penalty for a second or
subsequent revoke by the same player in
the same suit.

☐ ☐

4 It is improper for a player to attempt to
conceal his revoke by continuing to fail to follow
on the subsequent play of the suit.

☐ ☐

5 You cannot correct a revoke after the trick
has been completed and turned.

☐ ☐

Answers

1 FALSE. There is no penalty for an established revoke, "if the
side that revoked did not win either the trick on which the revoke
occurred or any subsequent trick." The penalty may be only one
trick if the revoking side wins only one subsequent to the revoke;
two tricks if two are won.

2 FALSE. The dummy may revoke, but if it does there is no
penalty.

3 TRUE. There is no penalty "if the revoke was a revoke in the
same suit by the same player."

4 TRUE. According to the "Proprieties," "There is no obligation
to draw attention to an inadvertent infringement of law by one's
own side; however, a player should not attempt to conceal such
an infringement, as by committing a second revoke, concealing a
card involved in a revoke, or mixing the cards prematurely."

5 FALSE. "A revoke in any of the first eleven tricks becomes
established when the offender or his partner leads or plays *to
the following* trick, or names or otherwise designates a card to be
so played, or makes a claim or concession of tricks orally or by
facing his hand." A revoke may be corrected before it becomes
established. See "Revokes Not Subject to Penalty."

Excerpts from the Laws of Contract Bridge

Lead Penalty When declarer may impose a lead penalty he may specify a suit and either require the lead of that suit or forbid the lead of that suit for as long as the opponent retains the lead. When in the following pages only a "lead penalty" is cited, declarer has these rights. There are some other cases in which declarer has some control over a defender's lead, but not so much. In such cases, the exact penalty will be specified.

Barred Player A player who is barred once, or for one round, must pass the next time it is his turn to bid; a player who is barred throughout must pass in every turn until the auction of the current deal is completed.

Waiver of Penalty When a player calls or plays over an illegal call or play by his right-hand opponent, he accepts the illegal call or play and waives a penalty. The game continues as though no irregularity had occurred.

Penalty Card A card illegally exposed by a defender must be left on the table, face up, until it is played; and it must be played at the first legal opportunity, whether in leading, following suit, or trumping. When a defender has a penalty card and his partner has the lead, declarer may require or forbid the partner to lead the suit of the penalty card; but if declarer does so, the card may be picked up and ceases to be a penalty card.

New Shuffle and Cut Before the first card is dealt, any player may demand a new shuffle and cut. There must be a new shuffle and cut if a card is faced in shuffling or cutting.

Deal Out of Turn   The correct dealer may reclaim the deal before the last card is dealt; thereafter, the deal stands as though it had been in turn and the correct dealer loses his right to deal in that round.

Redeal   There must be a redeal if the cards are not dealt correctly; if the pack is incorrect; if a card is faced in the pack or elsewhere; if a player picks up the wrong hand and looks at it; or if at any time during the play one hand is found to have too many cards and another too few (and the discrepancy is not caused by errors in play). When there is a redeal, the same dealer deals (unless the deal was out of turn) and with the same pack, after a new shuffle and cut.

Incorrect Hand   If a player has too few cards and the missing card is found (except in a previous trick), it is considered to have been in the short hand throughout. If it cannot be found, there is a redeal. If it is found in a previous trick, see Defective Trick.

Enforcing a Penalty   Either opponent (but not the dummy) may select or enforce a penalty. If partners consult as to selection or enforcement, the right to penalize is canceled.

Card Exposed During the Auction   No penalty for exposing a single card lower than a ten. If the exposed card is an honor, or any card prematurely led, or more than one card, each exposed card must be left face up on the table; the partner of the offender must pass at his next turn; and each exposed card becomes a penalty card if the other side plays the hand.

Change of Call   A player may change a call without penalty if he does so without pause. Any other attempted change of call is canceled. If the first call was an illegal call, it is subject to the applicable law; if it was a legal call, the offender may either:

(a) allow his first call to stand, whereupon his partner must pass at his next turn; or

(b) substitute any legal call (including a pass, double, or redouble), whereupon his partner must pass at every subsequent turn.

Insufficient Bid If a player makes an insufficient bid, he must substitute either a sufficient bid or a pass (not a double or redouble). If he substitutes:

(a) the lowest sufficient bid in the same denomination, there is no penalty.

(b) any other bid, partner must pass at all subsequent turns.

(c) a pass, his partner must pass at every subsequent turn, and declarer (if an opponent) may impose a lead penalty. A double or redouble illegally substituted is penalized the same as a pass and is treated as a pass.

The offender need not select his final call until the law has been stated; previous attempts at correction are canceled.

Information Given in Changing Call A denomination named, then canceled, in making or correcting an illegal call, is subject to penalty if an opponent becomes declarer: If a suit was named, declarer may impose a lead penalty; if notrump was named, declarer may call a suit, if the offender's partner has the opening lead; if a double or redouble was canceled, the penalties are the same as when a pass is substituted for an insufficient bid.

Call Out of Rotation (or "Out of Turn") Any call out of rotation is canceled when attention is drawn to it. The auction reverts to the player whose turn it was. Rectification and penalty depend on whether it was a pass, a bid, or a double or redouble, as follows:

A call is not out of rotation if made without waiting for the right-hand opponent to pass, if that opponent is legally obliged to pass; nor if it would have been in rotation had not the left-hand opponent called out of rotation. A call made simultaneously with another player's call in rotation is deemed to be subsequent to it.

Pass Out of Turn If it occurs (a) before any player has

bid, or when it was the turn of the offender's right-hand opponent, the offender must pass when his regular turn comes; (b) after there has been a bid and when it was the turn of the offender's partner, the offender is barred throughout; the offender's partner may not double or redouble at that turn; and if the offender's partner passes and the opponents play the hand, declarer may impose a lead penalty.

Bid Out of Turn If it occurs (a) before any player has called, the offender's partner is barred throughout; (b) after any player has called and when it was the turn of the offender's partner, the offender's partner is barred throughout and is subject to a lead penalty if he has the opening lead; (c) after any player has called and when it was the turn of the offender's right-hand opponent, the offender must repeat his bid without penalty if that opponent passes, but if that opponent bids the offender may make any call and his partner is barred once.

Double or Redouble Out of Turn If it occurs (a) when it was the turn of the offender's partner, the offender's partner is barred throughout and is subject to a lead penalty if he has the opening lead, and the offender may not in turn double or redouble the same bid; (b) when it was the turn of the offender's right-hand opponent, the offender must repeat his double or redouble without penalty if that opponent passes but may make any legal call if that opponent bids, in which case the offender's partner is barred once.

Impossible Doubles and Redoubles If a player doubles or redoubles a bid that his side has already doubled or redoubled, his call is canceled; he must substitute (a) any legal bid, in which case his partner is barred throughout and if he becomes the opening leader declarer may prohibit the lead of the doubled suit; or (b) a pass, in which case either opponent may cancel all previous doubles and redoubles, the offender's partner is barred throughout, and if he leads first is subject to a lead penalty.

If a player doubles his partner's bid, redoubles an undoubled bid, or doubles or redoubles when there has been no bid, he must substitute any proper call, and his partner is barred once.

Other Inadmissible Calls If a player bids more than seven, or makes another call when legally required to pass, he is deemed to have passed and the offending side must pass at every subsequent turn; if they become the defenders, a declarer may impose a lead penalty on the opening leader.

Call After the Auction is Closed A call made after the auction is closed is canceled. If it is a pass by a defender, or any call by declarer or dummy, there is no penalty. If it is a bid, double or redouble by a defender, declarer may impose a lead penalty at the offender's partner's first turn to lead.

Dummy's Rights Dummy may give or obtain information regarding fact or law, ask if a play constitutes a revoke (renege), draw attention to an irregularity, and warn any player against infringing a law. Dummy forfeits these rights if he looks at a card in another player's hand.

If dummy has forfeited his rights, and thereafter

(a) is the first to draw attention to a defender's irregularity, declarer may not enforce any penalty for the offense;

(b) warns declarer not to lead from the wrong hand, either defender may choose the hand from which declarer shall lead;

(c) is the first to ask declarer if a play from declarer's hand is a revoke, declarer must correct a revoke if able but the revoke penalty still applies.

Exposed Cards Declarer is never subject to penalty for exposure of a card, but intentional exposure of declarer's hand is treated as a claim or concession of tricks.

A defender's card is exposed if it is faced on the table or held so that the other defender may see its face before he is entitled to do so. Such a card must be left face up on the table until played and becomes a penalty card.

Penalty Cards A penalty card must be played at the first legal opportunity, subject to the obligation to follow suit or to comply with another penalty.

If a defender has two or more penalty cards that he can legally play, declarer may designate which one is to be played.

Declarer may require or forbid a defender to lead a suit in which his partner has a penalty card, but if declarer does so the penalty card may be picked up and ceases to be a penalty card.

Failure to play a penalty card is not subject to penalty, but declarer may require the penalty card to be played and any defender's card exposed in the process becomes a penalty card.

Lead Out of Turn If declarer is required by a defender (a defender's drawing attention to declarer's lead from the wrong hand is equivalent to requiring its retraction) to retract a lead from the wrong hand, he must lead from the correct hand (if he can) a card of the same suit; if it was a defender's turn to lead, or if there is no card of that suit in the correct hand, there is no penalty.

If a defender is required to retract a lead out of turn, declarer may either treat the card so led as a penalty card, or impose a lead penalty on the offender's partner when next he is to lead after the offense.

Premature Play If a defender leads to the next trick before his partner has played to the current trick, or plays out of rotation before his partner has played, declarer may require the offender's partner to play his highest card of the suit led, his lowest card of the suit led, or a card of another specified suit. Declarer must select one of these options and if the defender cannot comply, he may play any card. When declarer has played from both his hand and dummy, a defender is not subject to penalty for playing before his partner.

Inability to Play as Required If a player is unable to lead or play as required to comply with a penalty (for lack of a card of a required suit, or because of the prior obligation to follow suit) he may play any card. The penalty is deemed satisfied, except in the case of a penalty card.

Revoke A revoke is the act of playing a card of another suit, when able to follow suit to a lead. Any player, including dummy, may ask whether a play constitutes a revoke and may demand that an opponent correct a revoke. A claim of revoke does not warrant inspection of turned tricks, prior to the end of play, except by consent of both sides.

Correcting a Revoke A player must correct his revoke if aware of it before it becomes established. A revoke card withdrawn by a defender becomes a penalty card. The non-offending side may withdraw any cards played after the revoke but before attention was drawn to it.

Established Revoke A revoke becomes established when a member of the offending side leads or plays to a subsequent trick (or terminates play by a claim or concession). When a revoke becomes established, the revoke trick stands as played (unless it is the twelfth trick—see below).

Revoke Penalty The penalty for an established revoke is two tricks (if available), transferred at the end of play from the revoking side to the opponents. This penalty can be paid only from tricks won by the revoking side after its first revoke, including the revoke trick. If only one trick is available, the penalty is satisfied by transferring one trick; if no trick is available, no penalty.

There is no penalty for a subsequent established revoke in the same suit by the same player.

A transferred trick ranks for all scoring purposes as a trick won in play by the side receiving it. It never affects the contract. (For example, if the contract is two hearts and declarer wins eight tricks plus two tricks as a revoke penalty, total ten tricks, he can score only sixty points below the line and the other sixty points go above the line.)

Revokes Not Subject to Penalty A revoke made in the twelfth trick must be corrected, without penalty, if discovered before the cards have been mixed together. The non-offending side may require the offender's partner to play either of two cards he could legally have played. A revoke not discovered until the cards have been mixed is not subject to penalty, nor is a revoke by any faced hand (dummy, or a defender's hand when faced in consequence of a claim by declarer). A revoke by failure to play a penalty card is not subject to the penalty for an established revoke.

Defective Trick A defective trick may not be corrected after a player of each side has played to the next trick. If a player has failed to play to a trick, he must correct his error when it is discovered by adding a card to the trick (if possible, one he could legally have played to it). If a player has played more than one card to a trick, he does not play to the last trick or tricks and if he wins a trick with his last card, the turn to lead passes to the player at his left.

Declarer Claiming or Conceding Tricks If declarer claims or concedes one or more of the remaining tricks (verbally or by spreading his hand), he must leave his hand face up on the table and immediately state his intended plan of play.

If a defender disputes declarer's claim, declarer must play on, adhering to any statement he has made, and in the absence of a specific statement he may not "exercise freedom of choice in making any play the success of which depends on finding either opponent with or without a particular unplayed card."

Following curtailment of play by declarer, it is permissible for a defender to expose his hand and to suggest a play to his partner.

Defender Claiming or Conceding Tricks A defender may show any or all of his cards to declarer to establish a claim or concession. He may not expose his hand to partner. If he does, declarer may treat his partner's cards as penalty cards.

Correcting the Score A proved or admitted error in any score may be corrected at any time before the rubber score is agreed, except as follows: An error made in entering or failing to enter a partscore, or in omitting a game or in awarding one, may not be corrected after the last card of the second succeeding correct deal has been dealt (unless a majority of the players consents).

Effect of Incorrect Pack Scores made as a result of hands played with an incorrect pack are not affected by the discovery of the imperfection after the cards have been mixed together.